60 0331614 8

A Teacher Training Course for Teachers of EFL
Trainee's Book

L. A. HILL and M. DOBBYN

Cassell
London

Cassell Ltd
1 St Anne's Road, Eastbourne, East Sussex BN21 3UN

First printed 1979
Reprinted 1983

ISBN 0 304 30371 2

331614

q

Typeset by Gloucester Typesetting Co. Ltd.
Printed in Great Britain by
Richard Clay (The Chaucer Press) Ltd
Bungay, Suffolk

Contents

Introduction

This book is part of Dr Hill's and Dr Dobbyn's *Teacher Training Course for Teachers of EFL*.

The first book (*Teacher Training Course: Lecturer's Book*) is for the people who train teachers of English as a foreign language. This book is for the people who are being trained as EFL teachers.

The purpose of the book is to give the trainee suggestions, things to think about and things to write about.

It can be used by people who are not having formal teacher training, as well as by ones who are.

And finally, it can also be used by those who are already EFL teachers but wish to give themselves a refresher course.

1 Ear and speech training

1.1 CONSONANT AND VOWEL SOUNDS

1.1.1 Suggestions for Teaching Practice

1 Choose two sounds which change the meaning of a word in English (these are called *sound contrasts*; see *Lecturer's Book*, 1.1.1) and which are difficult for your pupils.

2 Make a list of pairs of words which are different only in those two sounds (these are called *minimal pairs*), and are easy to demonstrate or to draw pictures of, e.g. for /i/ and /e/:

    sitting – setting (of the sun)
    bill   – bell
    pin   – pen
    tin   – ten

3 Choose three pairs of words from your list and use them to give a test to find out whether a particular class has difficulties with them (see *Lecturer's Book*, 1.1.2).

4 Use four of the pairs for ear training (see *Lecturer's Book*, 1.1.3).

5 Use four of the pairs for speech training (see *Lecturer's Book*, 1.1.4).

6 Choose two other sounds which change meaning in English and again make a list of pairs of words.

7 Use some of them to build up a complete ear and speech training lesson of about fifteen minutes. The steps should be:

   (a) test to find out whether the class has trouble with these sounds
   (b) ear training
   (c) speech training
   (d) speech testing (see *Lecturer's Book*, 1.1.5).

1.1.2 Suggestions for Preparing Materials for Class

1 Choose one vowel contrast which your pupils find difficult.

Draw four pairs* of simple pictures to practise the contrast, e.g.:

> a man *sleeping* and another man *slipping*
> a dog *bitten* by a man and a dog *beaten* by a man.

2   Choose a consonant contrast which your pupils find difficult. Cut out four pairs* of pictures from newspapers or magazines which show the contrast, e.g.:

> *three* and a *tree*
> a *path* and a *part* (of something).

3   Write a list of pairs for either a vowel or a consonant contrast on a big piece of paper or cardboard** which you can put up in the classroom and which all the pupils can see.

For more information see L. A. Hill, *Drills and Tests*, sections 1–63.

1.2   CONSONANT CLUSTERS

1.2.1   Suggestions for Teaching Practice

1   Choose one difficult cluster and say a word which contains it to each pupil in turn. Ask him to repeat it, and then go on to the next pupil. Make sure that your lips can be seen clearly, that you are looking at the pupil and that he/she is looking at you. Repeat the drill at a distance of about five metres, and finally as if the pupils were at the back of a large class. Try not to lose contact with them.

2   As in 1 above, but work with one pupil only, giving him words containing different clusters.

3   Explain orally, and as simply and as shortly as you can, how to pronounce clusters which are made up of a plosive*** +/w/ or /l/. Try to use only words and ideas which a pupil in the classes which you are going to teach could understand.

4   As in 3 above, but this time explain how to pronounce clusters which are made up of a voiceless consonant /p/, /t/, /k/, /s/, /ʃ/, /f/ or /θ/, followed by a voiced one, /l/, /m/, /n/, /r/, /j/ or /w/.

5   Choose some clusters, some at the beginning of words (*initial*) and some at the end (*final*). Divide these clusters into the separate consonant phonemes of which they are made up.

* If you cannot find pairs like these (minimal pairs), then choose single words, and draw separate pictures (not in pairs) for them.
** One meter by 75cms is a good size for a class of 30 students.
*** /p/, /t/, /k/, /b/ or /g/

Make sure the pupils can pronounce each consonant by itself. Then teach the clusters you have chosen. You may choose three easy clusters, so that the pupils will get used to the method you are using before they have to practise the difficult ones.

VARIATIONS

6 Difficult clusters such as /pl/, /fj/ and /skr/ can sometimes be taught by introducing them between two separate words, then pronouncing the words very close together and finally pronouncing the cluster at the beginning of the second word, e.g. for /pl/, /fj/ and /skr/, one can have:

shéep land .... shé planned
if yóu .... a féw
this créw .... the scréw.

1.2.2 Suggestions for Preparing Materials for Class

1 Find words containing clusters which are easy to illustrate with a picture cut from a magazine or a simple drawing. Collect as many such pictures as possible and stick them on cardboard, or prepare them in such a way that they can be used with a flannelboard or plastigraph.

2 Collect examples of sentences which, though natural, contain the same consonant cluster several times, e.g.:

Strong string will not stretch.

1.2.3 Suggestions for Teaching with Teams of Teachers

1 Divide up the work between three trainees as follows:

(a) finding out which clusters need to be taught
(b) drilling the separate consonants which are parts of a cluster
(c) teaching the clusters.

2 One trainee can teach the lesson while the others move round the room and check the pupils' attempts to imitate the teacher.

For more information see " 'Initial Clusters' and 'Final Clusters' " in L. A. Hill, *Selected Articles on the Teaching of English as a Foreign Language*, pp. 56–69.

1.3 SOUNDS AND SPELLINGS

1.3.1 Teaching Practice – Choosing What to Teach

If you look at some of your pupils' written work, you will see which relationships between sounds and spellings they have trouble with. Make a list of these.

1.3.2 Test to Find Out Whether You Have Chosen the Right Relationships for Your Lists

Give the pupils a short test to see which of the items you have chosen give them the most difficulty (see *Lecturer's Book*, 1.3.2).

1.3.3 Discussion of the Problem

This is the most important part of the lesson. The purpose is to show the pupils the different sounds which can be represented by the same letter. Work as follows:

1 Give examples of the various sounds. If you choose, for example, the letter *g*, you can point out that the words *page*, *get* and *sign* all contain *g*, but that it represents three different sounds – /dʒ/, /g/ and /ɸ/.

2 Remind the pupils of the others ways *g* behaves. Examples can be found in L. A. Hill, *English Sounds and Spellings*.

3 Explain that you will now talk about what happens to *g* when it is in front of *e* or *i*. Give examples of the commonest pronunciation in this position (*page, cages, giraffe, engine*) first. Then go on to the less common ones (*get, girl, give, tiger; garage, sabotage*). Make sure you write the words which behave in the same way on one part of the blackboard and those which behave in another way on another part of the board.

4 Do everything you can to make the pupils look *carefully* at the spellings. It is not enough for them just to stare at the blackboard. The pupils must make some active response if they are to fix the spellings in their minds. Above all, they must look away from the word and then try to spell it out, either in their mind or on paper.

1.3.4 Progress Test

Give the pupils the original test again, or a similar one which contains both words from the original test and new words.

1.3.5 Follow-up

Later you can give a dictation to help the pupils remember the work you have done. L. A. Hill's *English Sounds and Spellings: Dictation Pieces* contains ninety pieces each of which deals with one particular kind of spelling difficulty.

You should, of course, revise the work you have done, not

only in the next lesson, but also when similar kinds of sound-spelling relationships are being taught. For example if you have done some work on *c*, this can later easily be brought in again in a lesson on *ck* and *k*. A rather different kind of test should be used for this. The pupils should be given a list of words containing, for example, the /k/ sound, but the words should be written leaving out the spelling of that sound:

un . . . le
an . . . le
ta . . . le

The pupils would then supply the missing *c*, *k* or *ck* each time.

1.3.6 Suggestions for Preparing Materials for Class

Younger children, and older ones whose mother tongue is not written in a Latin alphabet, write so slowly that they sometimes forget, or become confused about, a spelling in the middle of writing a word down. If you have a set of *small* cards with letters ready printed on them, they can help here. Young pupils like arranging letters in the correct order, and it is a good exercise for fixing their attention on the spelling of a word.

For more information see L. A. Hill and J. M. Ure, *English Sounds and Spellings* and *English Sounds and Spellings: Tests*. Also L. A. Hill, *English Sounds and Spellings: Dictation Pieces*.

1.4 STRESS, RHYTHM AND INTONATION: EAR TRAINING

1.4.1 Preparing Yourself

STRESS

1   Practise repeating the same sentence over and over again without any change in the stress (or intonation) pattern. This is quite difficult to do, but you must be able to do it.

2   For this, you need two copies of the same story. Get one of your fellow-trainees to mark the stresses on his copy, and then dictate one sentence at a time, once only, while you listen and mark the stresses he uses. You will find that there is a particular speed (neither *too* fast nor *too* slow) at which it is easiest to do this. Practise reading examples at this speed yourself.

3   Write a sentence on the blackboard. Read it out aloud over and over again, marking one new 'hat' (o) each time (see *Lecturer's Book*, 1.4.1.2 and 1.4.1.3). Finally put the primary stress (′) in place of one of the 'hats' (rub this 'at' out first). Face away from the board while you are reading.

INTONATION

4   As in **1** above, read the same sentence over and over again without any change in the intonation pattern.

5   Practise the exact words you will use to explain how the intonation tails rise and fall after the primary stress. Make sure you have good examples ready. Explain everything in language that an ordinary pupil can understand.

6   As in **5** above, but this time talk about how to choose between high or low pitch at the start of the intonation head.

7   As in **5** above, but talk about how the steps down occur.

1.4.2   Practice Teaching

You should probably not spend more than fifteen or twenty minutes at a time on any part of stress, rhythm or intonation. Plan your teaching so that you can do this. This means preparing other things to do during the rest of the lesson.

1   STRESS COMPARED WITH NO STRESS: Prepare six examples. Write them on the blackboard. Read them to the pupils, and ask them to tell you where the stresses fall. You may wish to get the pupils to copy the last two sentences and to mark the stresses on them at their desks. You can then go through these two on the board.

2   PRIMARY COMPARED WITH SECONDARY STRESS: Revise the six sentences used in **1** above and then ask the pupils to change one of the 'hats' into a primary stress mark (see *Lecturer's Book*, 1.4.1.3). Be careful not to change the stress you use in your readings of the same sentence. You may wish to go through the examples again, telling the pupils that this time you will put the primary stress on a different word and, of course, doing so.

3   PREPARATORY TEST, to find out how well pupils can hear intonation: Many pupils have difficulty in recognizing high and low pitch. A very few cannot do it at all. We must help the first kind and find out who are of the second. Before starting on examples of difference in pitch in speech, we can demonstrate *high* and *low* by bringing two glasses which are exactly the same into class and filling one to the top and the other to a lower level with water and then hitting each gently with a pencil. Next we can keep the two glasses out of sight and, after hitting them both, ask which one we tapped first. This is an exercise in which the pupils can work in small groups. This brightens up an exercise which many pupils find both difficult and dull.

4   RISING AND FALLING INTONATION: Choose six statements which can be turned into questions by a change in the intonation pattern, e.g.:

> Tomorrow is a holiday.
> Tomorrow is a holiday?

Write them on the board without punctuation. Read each of them either as a statement or as a question, and ask the class to tell you whether you have used rising or falling pitch, and where it begins. You can teach intonation tails in this way.

5   Revise 4 above, and then teach how the intonation heads are formed (see *Lecturer's Book*, 1.4.1.4).

6   Write four sentences on the board. Mark the stress yourself. Ask the class to mark the intonation, including the steps down in the head.

7   You can usefully spend ten minutes revising 1 to 6 above after the ear training has been finished.

8   Do not forget that coloured chalk can be very useful in teaching both stress and intonation. If you use it, you may find that it is best to write the original sentences in a 'quiet' colour, like green or red, and to keep white for the stress and intonation marks.

1.4.3   Suggestions for Preparing Materials for Class

1   Prepare a tape of the examples you are going to use. To find an example on the tape, you must either make a very careful note of the number at which the example starts on the tape, or mark the tape itself. This can be done with a yellow wax crayon, and it can be rubbed out afterwards. A felt-tip pen will also in some cases mark the tape, but it is not so easy to remove.

2   Use carbon paper, or a copying machine of some kind if you have one, to prepare worksheets which you can then distribute to the pupils. The sheets should contain the exercises which are to be done in class, i.e. the sentences, without the stress and intonation marks, which you will read to the pupils.

3   Write each of the words of one of the sentences you will be using on a separate postcard. Prepare the cards for use with a flannelboard. When you want to demonstrate the shape of the

intonation pattern, you can simply lift or lower each card so that the sentence itself has a rising or a falling shape.

1.4.4   Suggestions for Teaching in Teams

1   For teaching stress, the lesson can easily be divided between two trainees. One teaches the pupils to recognize stressed syllables. The other teaches them to recognize primary stress.

2   For teaching intonation, one trainee should teach the pupils to recognize rising and falling ends of sentences; one should teach the rules of intonation heads and tails; and a third can teach them about steps down in the head.

3   Instead of 1 and 2, for both stress and intonation, one trainee can do all the teaching and demonstrating. The rest of the trainees in his group can check the pupils' work. If a tape-recorder is used, one trainee should, of course, be in charge of using it.

For more information see L. A. Hill, *Stress and Intonation Step by Step: Workbook* and *Stress and Intonation Step by Step: Companion.*

1.5   STRESS, RHYTHM AND INTONATION: SPEECH TRAINING

1.5.1   Suggestions for Teaching

Many of the drills suggested for **1.4** (Stress, Rhythm and Intonation: Ear Training) are suitable for speech training. The jobs of teacher and pupil are, of course, changed over: the pupil speaks and the teacher listens. In addition, however, the following may be used:

1   Make up some sentences which can give your pupils practice in speaking with good stress, rhythm and intonation (see *Lecturer's Book*, 1.4.2).

2   Present the sentences to the class in the following order:

(a)   read the phrase aloud several times clearly and with good rhythm, slightly over-emphasizing the stress pattern
(b)   do the same as in (a), but also tap with a ruler
(c)   tell the pupils to join in the tapping (fingers only, please!)
(d)   continue tapping, but switch to 'da da da's'
(e)   tell the pupils to join in
(f)   change back to the real words of the sentence
(g)   tell the pupils to join in.

3   Make up six sentences which have the same stress and intonation patterns. Read them over to your fellow-trainees without changing the intonation pattern as you go through the list. Here is a set. Try to find others.

It's tîme the pûpils stôpped their wórk.

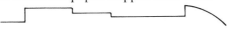

> I hear them packing up their books.
> They have to leave the school at four.
> We really shouldn't keep them late.
> It gets quite dark by ten to five.
> And some have quite a way to go.

4   Count slowly to the pupils the numbers from sixteen to twenty-five. Tap with a ruler to show where the stresses come. (They change at *twenty-one*.) Then ask the pupils to tap with you, and finally to count with you. Because the numbers are familiar to them, they will be able to give all their attention to the stress pattern. This exercise takes no account of which stress is primary.

5   Repeat exercise **4**, but this time use the numbers from one to six. The first time you count the group of numbers, put the primary stress on the last one in the group. Next time put it on *five*. Next time on *four* and so on. Make the pupils repeat the group after you each time. This will train them to distinguish the primary stress from the other stresses:

> Ône, twô, thrêe, fôur, fíve, síx
> Ône, twô, thrêe, fôur, fíve, sîx (etc.).

6   (Stress compared with no stress, and primary stress compared with secondary stress)   Choose four examples of the same stress pattern. Then, with each in turn:

(a)   say it several times to the pupils
(b)   ask them to repeat it, first with you and then after you, while you check that they are not stressing any unstressed syllables
(c)   as in (b), but check that they have the primary stress in the right place
(d)   ask individual pupils to read it, without your model, from the board.

7   (Preparatory pitch exercise)   Use only 'da, da, da's'. Give pupils varying combinations of high and low 'da's' and ask them to repeat them after you. For example:

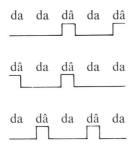

da   da   dâ   da   dâ

dâ   da   dâ   da   da

da   dâ   da   dâ   da

Work first with groups and then with individuals. Now ask for varying combinations without giving the model: say 'high, low, high', or 'low, low, high'. This is also a good exercise for work in small groups.

8   (Rising and falling glides) Review **2** above first. Then work with short sentences which can be either statements or questions according to the intonation pattern of the tail (see **1.4.2.4**).

9   (Intonation heads and steps down) Review **2** above first. Then work with phrases which are different only because of the shape of the head. Here are examples:

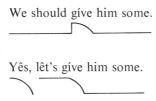

We should gíve him some.

Yês, lêt's gíve him some.

10   (Steps down) For more concentrated practice of steps down, longer sentences are needed. They should not, however, become difficult simply because of their length, or the pupils will have so many problems of vocabulary and grammar that they will not be able to concentrate on stress and intonation. One good way is to use a sentence which builds up each time it is repeated. One of the best is *The house that Jack built.* As each line comes, more things, and therefore more steps down, are added, e.g.:

Thîs is the hôuse that Jáck bûilt.

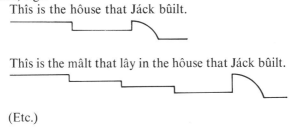

Thîs is the mâlt that lây in the hôuse that Jáck bûilt.

(Etc.)

1.5.2   Suggestions for Preparing Materials for Class

1   Make sure that your copy of *everything* that you are going to use is fully marked for stress and intonation. You may need to write out your examples on larger paper than usual, or at least more widely spaced out on the usual paper.

2   If you have not lived long in the country that your pupils come from, you may miss chances of teaching stress and intonation by the use of simple instruments which are familiar to the children. Hardly any culture is without some simple drum or, more useful, set of drums.

For more information see L. A. Hill, *Stress and Intonation Step by Step: Workbook* and *Stress and Intonation Step by Step: Companion.*

2 Oral presentation and drill (teaching new items)

2.1 LEXICAL ITEMS (WORDS AND FORMULAS)

A teacher could not, of course, spend a whole lesson on presenting and drilling new items. Almost all teaching of vocabulary items will, therefore, be micro-teaching. Nor is there any place for team teaching.

2.1.1 Micro-Teaching Suggestions

TEACHING BY DEMONSTRATION

1   The following six items are suitable for teaching by demonstration. Demonstrate *one* meaning of each item in a way that a class of *beginners* (one or two years of English only) could easily understand (see *Lecturer's Book*, 2.2.1). Try to use only items which you would easily find in the classroom. For example:

> beyond, past, above, over, in front of, before.

2   The following six items are suitable for teaching by demonstration to an *intermediate* class. Demonstrate *one* meaning of each verb. You will probably have to do a bit of acting. You will also be tempted to add definitions to your demonstrations. Try not to add these.

> answer, argue, listen, hear, wait, expect.

TEACHING BY PICTURES

3   Find a picture or pictures, or even draw your own if you can, and use them to teach six vocabulary items, suitable for *beginners*, which describe ordinary life. Here are some suggestions:

> a church or a mosque, a football match, a factory,
> a railway station, a cheque or some money.

4   Find a picture or pictures of six actions, and use them to teach the items to an *intermediate* class. Here are some suggestions:

> making a phone call, going on a picnic, watching
> television, having a meal with friends, shopping.

TEACHING BY CONTEXT

For each of the following sets of lexical items it is easy to think of a context into which they will fit. The context may be a reference to some real thing that has happened recently, or to some common subject of children's stories, or perhaps you may prefer to write a story yourself.

5   *Beginners' level*

sea, submarine, wreck, treasure, diver, vanish.

6   *Intermediate level*

gaol, prisoner, escape, reward, trail, arrest.

7   *Advanced level*

guerrilla, hijack, hostage, ransom, dynamite, negotiate.

TEACHING BY TRANSLATION
Giving the meaning of a word by translating it is, in many ways, so easy that useful micro-teaching exercises become hard to find. Also, the difficulty of finding a good translation for any particular English word will vary from mother-tongue to mother-tongue. We have therefore chosen groups of words which, in English, differ from each other only slightly. Your mother-tongue may have either more or less words than the English language has to cover the same area of meaning. Your job is to decide in which ways you will use the available mother-tongue words to translate those in the following lists:

8   *Advanced level*

skilful, clever, quick-witted, intelligent, intellectual.

9   *Advanced level*

regular, reliable, trustworthy, honest, straightforward.

TEACHING BY DEFINITION
Definition is the easiest means for a bad teacher. He thinks he has defined the item well whatever he says. He has little feed-back from the pupils except a repetition of his own definition. If you use definition as a method of presenting the meaning of a word, follow these steps, which will prevent you from leaving your class completely puzzled:

(a)   Say the word several times in a clear voice so that the pupils know which word you are talking about.
(b)   Write it up on the board and say it again. Make the pupils repeat it.
(c)   Give several examples. This will make the pupils form some ideas of their own. It will also make them curious to know whether they have guessed correctly or not.

(d)   Define the meaning of the word as best you can. Make sure that your definition, whether it is a good one or a bad one, is at least one which the pupils can understand.

(e)   Give more examples of the word in context. Ask the pupils for examples. (It is safe to do this now; you must not do it earlier.)

(f)   Call attention to the spelling and tell the pupils to write the word somewhere (the best place is in their vocabulary notebooks).

10   Here are some words suitable for presentation by definition at an *advanced* level:

>   an optimist, a strike, a vice-president, pollution,
>   a telescope, a by-pass, a barometer, a fire-extinguisher.

11   Remember that many words have several different meanings: a *spring* can be a coiled piece of metal as well as water coming out of a rock. In elementary classes we usually want to teach one meaning at a time; but in more advanced classes we can often save time by explaining several different meanings of the same word when it first comes up for discussion. Providing contexts for each meaning is not easy, but it must be done. Look at the following items and decide which meaning you would teach first; and which other meanings, if any, you would teach at the same time (a) in a beginner's class, and (b) in an advanced class:

>   top, bill, ball, feed
>   turn off, turn down
>   call for, call (someone) (something).

During all your micro-teaching work ask your fellow trainees to check the following:

(a)   Have you presented the meaning of the word as it appeared in the context where you met it?

(b)   Have you presented the form of the word (noun, adjective, etc.) which appeared in that context?

(c)   Have you taught the spelling and pronunciation of the word?

2.2   PATTERNS

2.2.1   Suggestions for Micro-Teaching

The presentation of grammatical patterns cannot easily be divided up into micro-teaching sections. The first few moments of each presentation, however, are extremely important. If the pupils clearly understand what new meaning the teacher is trying to deal with, what new patterns he is introducing, and how a change in meaning corresponds to a change in pattern – if the pupils understand these things quickly, three-quarters of the teacher's task is done. The trainee must, therefore, be absolutely sure how to start off his presentation. We therefore recommend that the first step in each of the following macro-teaching suggestions should be separated off and practised on its own.

2.2.2 Suggestions for Macro-Teaching

The teaching of patterns, more than any other thing in language teaching, is dependent upon what has already been taught. One would be foolish to try to teach *She said Napoleon was a hero* before the pupils have learnt *She said "Good morning"* and *Napoleon is a hero*. For this reason, we give here a variety of patterns for the trainees to choose from. The first few patterns listed are fairly simple ones. The last few are harder. Before deciding which patterns to choose for practice teaching, the trainee should make sure of what his pupils already know.

There are three main types of difficulty which the pupils will have when they are learning the patterns of English: problems of function words (e.g. *if*, *when*, *but*), problems of word order (e.g. *I do not think he will die*, but *I hope he will not die*), and problems of inflexion (e.g. *James forgot his homework*, but *Sue forgot her homework*). Suggestions follow in each of these three areas.

FUNCTION WORDS

1 Here are some patterns in which the word *enough* is important:

(a) It is *enough*.
(b) It is long *enough*.
(c) It is long *enough* for me.
(d) It is long *enough* for me to use.
(e) It is long *enough* to reach the end.

2 There are many simple classroom situations in which these patterns can be presented. Here are a few:

(a) Bring in a small parcel and a piece of string. Is the string *enough* if you want to tie up the parcel? Is it long *enough*?
(b) Ask a small boy to give you his coat. Give it to a big boy and tell him to put it on. Is it big *enough* for him? Is it big *enough* for him to wear?
(c) Ask a pupil to work out a mathematical sum. Meanwhile tell another pupil to count to twenty while the first pupil

is doing his sum. Is the time long *enough* for him to work
out the sum?

Use these situations to demonstrate the meaning of *enough*,
and to practise the patterns given above.

3   Here are some more difficult patterns using *enough*:
   (a)   I have *enough* string.
   (b)   I have *enough* string for the parcel.
   (c)   The string is not nearly *enough*.
   (d)   There is nothing like *enough* string (for me) (to do the
         job).

The classroom situations suggested in exercise **2** can be used
again.

WORD ORDER

1   The words *sometimes*, *always* and *never* are in a different position in the pattern when it is a *be* pattern from the position they
are in when the verb is one like *come* and *go*. Here are some
patterns with a place for *sometimes/always/never*:

   (a)   Willy is *never* late.
   (b)   Willy is *never* late on Mondays.
   (c)   Willy *never* comes late on Mondays.
   (d)   Probably he will *never* come late next year.
   (e)   Does he *never* come late?

2   Here are some classroom situations which can be used for
presenting and drilling these patterns:

   (a)   (Write the class timetable on the blackboard or, if each
         pupil has a copy, ask them to take it out and look at it.)
         Do we *never* have English on Fridays? No, we *never* have
         English on Fridays.
   (b)   (Point to an empty desk.) Peter is absent. Is he *always*
         absent? Who is *never* absent? etc.
   (c)   (Tell the pupils that they may talk quietly. Then ask them
         if they are usually allowed to talk in class.) Are they
         always allowed to talk? Are they *never* allowed to talk?
         etc.
   (d)   (Ask a difficult question. Ask the same pupil another
         difficult question.) Is he *sometimes* able to answer, or is
         he *never* able to answer? (Ask some easy questions.) Are
         the pupils *always* able to answer?
   (e)   Divide the pupils into pairs. Tell one of them to describe
         his day since he woke up. The other pupil in each pair
         should ask him questions about each action he describes,
         using either *always*, *sometimes* or *never*:

A I got up at seven o'clock.
B Do you *always* get up at seven o'clock?
A No, I *sometimes* get up at six o'clock.
B Do you *never* get up at eight o'clock?
A Yes, I *sometimes* get up at eight o'clock.

INFLEXIONS
Elementary level
(Substituting pronouns for nouns: correct agreement)
Ask three or four pupils to come up to the blackboard and give them each a piece of chalk. Ask them to draw a simple picture, with each pupil drawing part of it. Look away while they are doing this. If they have drawn a man on a bicycle, for example, you can ask one of the other members of the class such questions as the following:

TEACHER Did Richard draw the front wheel?
PUPIL   No, *he* didn't draw *it*.
TEACHER Did Paul draw the front wheel?
PUPIL   Yes, *he* drew *it*.
TEACHER (To Paul) Did you also draw the back wheel?
PAUL   Yes, I drew *it*.
TEACHER (To Paul) So, you drew both wheels?
PAUL   Yes, I drew *them*.

With a little thought and preparation, this drill can go on in an interesting way round the class so as to practise most of the pronouns. The pupils must, of course, also have a chance to *ask* questions. This is very important indeed.

Intermediate level
Here is a set of tag-question patterns:

(a) It's Wednesday, *isn't it*?
(b) It isn't Thursday, *is it*?
(c) Yesterday was Tuesday, *wasn't it*?
(d) Tomorrow will be Thursday, *won't it*?
(e) Tomorrow won't be Friday, *will it*?

The patterns can all be drilled together, or one or two can be chosen for presentation together. Of course you must change the days of the week in the examples so that they make sense on the day you present the patterns.

Start by making some remark such as, "Today is Wednesday, so I want your compositions." Some pupil is certain to protest, "No, *yesterday* was Wednesday." The rest of the presentation will follow naturally.

There are several ways in which role-playing can be used to present and drill these patterns. The teacher should begin the game and let the pupils take over when they understand. Here is an example:

An anxious mother is giving advice to her little girl.

MOTHER   You won't come back late, *will you*?
GIRL   No, I won't.
MOTHER   You will be able to find the way, *won't you*?
GIRL   Yes, I will.
MOTHER   The house is number six, *isn't it*? (Etc.)

A variation of the above is for the story-teller to pause after each event. The listener then guesses what came next:

STORY-TELLER   Then what do you think I did?
LISTENER   You turned and ran, *didn't you*?

2.2.3 Suggestions for Preparing Materials for Class

The materials you will need depend upon the situations you choose in which to present the patterns. If you choose the parcel-and-string presentation of *The string is not long enough* you must have a small parcel and a piece of string. This advice seems obvious, but many teachers wrongly believe that if they pretend to have a parcel and pretend to have a piece of string, all will be well. It may be, but more often the pupils will simply pretend to understand.

2.2.4 Suggestions for Team Teaching

If you practise carefully with your fellow-trainees before the presentation, they can be of great help to you. They can, for example, provide the situation you need, showing that the coat belonging to one of them is *not big enough* for the other to wear. They can act out the little situations, the mother and the daughter (or father and son, if the trainees are all male), etc.

3 Aural comprehension

3.1 SUGGESTIONS FOR MICRO-TEACHING

The three important phases in an aural comprehension lesson are:

(1) a good reading of the story
(2) questions which are well presented in simple language
(3) a good way of dealing with the pupils' answers, both the right ones and the wrong ones.

Each of these three activities can be carried out more efficiently with practice.

Here are some suggestions for work with your fellow trainees:

Reading a story

1 Read the story you choose to your fellow trainees, several times over. There are five things you should concentrate on. You will not be able to think of them all at once, but you can watch one or two of them each time you read the story.

   (a) Check your position while you are reading. You should be standing, holding the book in your left hand with your right thumb marking the line you are on. Read one phrase, memorize it, *look up at the class* and start to say the phrase. Towards the end of the phrase look down again at the book. Memorize the next phrase during the pause. Look up again, and so on to the end.
   (b) Check the speed at which you read. The speed should vary from section to section of the story in order to hold the pupils' interest. It should not vary in the middle of a sentence, however. There should be pauses only at the end of sense groups.
   (c) Try to vary the pitch of your voice in order to show who is speaking in the story.
   (d) Remember to show the meaning of what you are reading with your face as well as with your words. Don't forget that your pupils are *watching* you in order to help understand what you are saying.
   (e) Do not be afraid of pausing for dramatic effect. The pauses must, of course, be in the right places. Properly

placed, however, a pause is invaluable as a way of letting the words sink into the pupils' minds.

Asking the questions

2   Whether the questions are handed out on paper, written on the board or asked orally, they will share certain qualities if they are good. These are:

(a) They should be designed to improve understanding. Questions in an aural comprehension lesson are designed to *help* rather than to test.

(b) The wording of the questions must be simple. Comprehension of the story is the aim, not comprehension of the questions about the story.

(c) They should be so designed that, provided the pupils have understood the story, the right answer is the most probable one to appear. Questions like, "What happened then?" can produce a variety of answers, even from pupils who fully understand the story. "What did the man show Mrs Stephens?" will produce the right answer.

(d) The English used in the questions must, of course, be good English and easy enough for the pupils to understand. Mistakes in the English used in the questions are not only confusing: they are also bad teaching.

Dealing with the answers

3   Both the right answer and the wrong answer are rather easy to deal with. The answer which is partly right and partly wrong is both more common and harder to do something about. Practise in groups the various ways of turning a partly correct answer into a correct one. The easiest way to do this is to ask a question, and get one of your fellow trainees to make a slight mistake (either in the English, or in the content) in replying. You must first accept, and praise, the correct part of the answer. You must then show exactly what part is incorrect and, by further questioning, direct the pupil towards a more correct answer.

3.2 SUGGESTIONS FOR MACRO-TEACHING

1   There are five different methods of presenting the questions to the pupils and receiving their answers: the questions can be oral or written ones; the answers can be oral or written; and if they are written, they may be of the free answer type or the multiple-choice type. Yet another technique is to allow the pupils to write as much of the story as they can remember. By combining the different possibilities we get five ways in which

we can carry the exercise out, as we shall see in a minute. The oral question followed by an oral answer is probably the most suitable for elementary classes. You can choose the technique most suited to the level of class you are given for practice teaching. It is, of course, most necessary to pick a story which is not only of the right standard of difficulty, but also has the right kind of subject. Girls usually like different stories from boys, and younger children like different stories from older ones. Adults again have their own preferred kinds of story.

2   We suggest that the procedures for each level should be as follows, though the practice teacher must suit his methods to the abilities of his pupils:

(a)   *Elementary level (I);* oral questions followed by oral answers
(b)   *Elementary level (II);* oral questions followed by written, multiple-choice type answers
(c)   *Intermediate level (I);* oral questions followed by free answers
(d)   *Intermediate level (II);* written questions followed by free written answers
(e)   *Advanced level;* the pupils should be asked to write as much of the story as they can remember.

3.3   SUGGESTIONS FOR THE PREPARATION OF MATERIALS FOR CLASS

1   For the multiple-choice type answers, suitable answer sheets will have to be prepared (see chapter 14 for more information on multiple-choice tests).

2   With many stories, simple visual aids are very useful. These should be pictures which are used to set the scene of the story, or to explain some unfamiliar object which appears in the story. They should not be illustrations of the events in the story, or visual comprehension will replace aural comprehension.

3.4   SUGGESTIONS FOR TEAM TEACHING

1   When listening to a new piece of dialogue, pupils often find it difficult to decide who is speaking at a particular moment. As a first step to helping them with this, two or more readers can share the reading of the story between them, one being the story-teller and the others reading the words of the different characters when they speak.

2   If several trainees are available, work in small groups is possible. One trainee can ask the questions, and the others can listen to the answers from several members of each group; or the questions can be written on the board, and all the trainees can act as group leaders. By such means, three or four times as many pupils have a chance to answer orally.

For more information see chapter 14, Tests and Examinations.

4 Oral work: oral composition using blackboard drawing

4.1 SUGGESTIONS FOR MICRO-TEACHING

1   The type of presentation we suggest depends for its success on the teacher being able to draw simple, clear pictures quickly. When the teacher's back is turned, naughty pupils sometimes cause trouble and even the best ones are unhappy when there are too many long pauses during the oral composition. Practise simple drawings of a house, a road, a few means of transport (boat, train, bicycle, car, etc.), and, above all, stick figures. Here is some advice which may help you:

(a)   *Stick figures*
Practise on lined paper. This will help you get the proportions right. The body should be about twice as long as the head, and the legs three times as long as the head. Practise first with the figure standing straight. When it is bent, you must, of course, shorten the parts accordingly. (See figures 1 and 2.)

Figure 1   **Figure 2**

(b)   *Nearer and farther*
If you want one figure to seem nearer than another, simply draw it larger than the one further away. (See figure 3.)

Figure 3

(c)   *Making things look solid*
Remember that all the parallel lines going away from you would meet in one point if they went on far enough (figure 4). The house will look even more realistic if you make all the parallel lines going from left to right also point to one spot. Usually this is not necessary unless you want to draw a long street (figures 5 and 6).

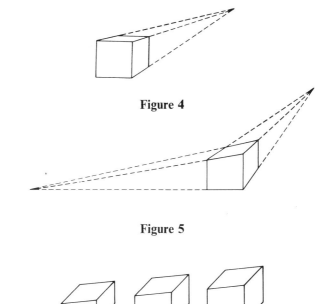

Figure 4

Figure 5

Figure 6

2   At first the teacher needs to help the pupils to give the right sentences by asking his questions in a suitable way. To get the answer, "He is holding a piece of paper in his hand" it is better to ask "What is he holding in his hand?" than "What is he doing?" You can practise careful phrasing of the questions you are going to ask to prompt the pupils. Here are some examples:

(a)   *A story in the past*
After going through a story once, using the present continuous tense, you may want the pupils, or a few of the better ones, to tell the story from memory. They cannot use the present continuous for this. How would you change the questions so as to produce:

      (1)   answers in the simple past (*He ran to the camp*) and

      (2)   answers in the past perfect (*He had seen smoke behind a bush*)?

      Would you need to show the pictures again for either of these changes in the time of the story?

(b)   '*What next?*'

      Another amusing variation is to show a picture and ask the pupils to guess what is likely to happen. This gives them practice in *The man will catch him* and *The man's going to catch him*. Once again, the answer will depend on the way the questions are put. Go through the story again, ask your questions in such a way that the *will catch* (or the *going to catch*) answers are likely to be given.

4.2 SUGGESTIONS FOR MACRO-TEACHING

1   Your first attempts at an oral composition lesson using the blackboard could usefully follow a model closely. If you have a copy of L. A. Hill's *Picture Composition Book*, you could start with the last set of pictures in that book (pp. 60 and 61). These pictures are accompanied by sample materials, a composition, test items and suggestions for teaching. Another suitable book is Donn Byrne's *Progressive Picture Compositions*.

VARIATIONS

2   Use either or both of the two techniques mentioned in **4.1.2** above to practise future and past forms.

3   Divide the class up into three or four groups and give one part of the story to each group. Everyone, of course, listens to the whole story, but when the time comes to retell it, each part of it is told by a separate group of pupils.

4   Use the picture composition series to practise commands and requests. The teacher says, "What shall I draw now?" and the class answers, "Draw him running to the camp." Negative commands can be brought in quite naturally, e.g. "Shall I make him fall?" "No, don't make him fall." This exercise is not quite an exercise in oral composition, but there are very few ways in which the pupils can be made to ask the teacher to do things, so the chance should not be missed.

5   When the story needs it, let the pupils supply the necessary dialogue.

4.3   SUGGESTIONS FOR THE PREPARATION OF MATERIALS FOR CLASS

If the scenes and figures to be used are prepared for use with a flannelboard or magnetic board, the lesson goes more quickly. The teacher is, however, far more restricted, and cannot take advantage of the enthusiastic suggestions from the class which often accompany good blackboard work.

4.4   SUGGESTIONS FOR TEAM TEACHING

1   The simplest division of work is for one trainee to draw the pictures while another is telling the story or questioning the class.

2   Instead, one trainee can go through the composition for the first time, using the present continuous tense. Another trainee can then do the follow-up work, asking the pupils to tell him what happened, using, of course, the past tense (see **4.1** above).

3   If there is enough blackboard space, each trainee can be responsible for a different scene or scenes, so that one picture is going up on the board while another is being used for the composition.

4   If the trainees do not mind being laughed at, it will be quite easy to arrange a little scene to be acted out by two or three of them. Stealing a watch from someone who is asleep, losing and finding something after looking in all the wrong places, going to the dentist and having a tooth pulled out, and many other little scenes can be used.

5 Oral work: conversation

5.1 SUGGESTIONS FOR MICRO-TEACHING

1 While we can suggest subjects for conversation, the success of a group discussion really depends upon the ability of the leader (the teacher) to keep things moving while not forcing too many of his own opinions on his class. "Keeping things moving" means (a) when a shy pupil says something, encouraging him to say more; and (b) discouraging pupils who talk too much, or who do not keep to the subject. Try the following pair of exercises to help you with these two activities:

(a) "That's a good idea. Can anyone think of some examples?"
"Perhaps you are right, but Jack looks as if he doesn't agree. Do you, Jack?"
Try to think of six more things you can say to encourage the pupils to develop an idea further, or to take more part in the conversation. (To see if your ideas work, wait until there is a discussion between your fellow trainees in their mother-tongue and then put in some of your remarks.)

(b) "What you say is true, but I'd like to see if the others feel differently."
"Maybe, but Jack looks as if he doesn't see what this has got to do with. . . ."
Try to think of six more things you can say to discourage people from going off the subject, or to prevent too much talk by one pupil. (Some of your remarks should be gentle, and some not so gentle. Try them during mother-tongue discussions, as above, to see their results.)

2 The kind of lesson which ends in confusion usually begins in confusion the next time. One weakness of conversation classes is that they seldom finish in a definite manner. A good summary by the teacher is one satisfactory way of finishing.

3 Practise, in your mother-tongue at first, the very difficult skill of listening to what is being said, and then presenting a short, summary of it. This does *not* mean giving your opinion on the subject: it means reporting faithfully what has been said. If you can do this well, you will give your pupils the feeling that what they think is interesting. It sometimes is. It often should be. It always should seem to be.

5.2   SUGGESTIONS FOR MACRO-TEACHING

1   Suitable subjects for conversation classes will be found in L. A. Hill's *Free Composition Book*, together with sets of questions for giving out to the pupils a few days in advance. Certain subjects are more suited to some groups than to others.

2   Most conversation is, in fact, carried on in order to exchange information or to be clearer about what the other person thinks, when one has only half understood it. This fact can be used to make conversation classes more natural. Ask half the class, for example, to read something – a story, a few paragraphs in a reference book, etc. – and then divide the class up into pairs so that a pupil who has not done the reading can question the other who has.

3   In the same way, if a subject is set for a composition, the work of collecting information for the composition can be divided up among members of the class, and the exchange of this information between pupils can be made the purpose of a conversation.

4   A conversation class is a good place for making use of the few exceptional pupils whom we sometimes find in a large group of average ones. The brighter members of the group can be given the job of keeping notes of what is said and making a summary, or preparing a report for the teacher, at the end of the discussion.

5.3   SUGGESTIONS FOR THE PREPARATION OF MATERIALS FOR CLASS

A particularly shy class can sometimes be persuaded to speak if some object such as a picture which deals with the subject is provided as a starting point. If the subject, for example, is *The advantages of life in a town*, a picture of a busy street scene may get the pupils to talk about the pleasures and the problems of city life. After choosing your conversation subject, try to find some suitable pictures.

5.4   SUGGESTIONS FOR TEAM TEACHING

Clearly, the smaller the group, the more chance each pupil has of talking. The class may be divided up into groups, each under a trainee, for either part or the whole of the conversation period.

6 Reading

6.1 PRACTICAL WORK

1 Visit either your college library or the local bookshop or, even better, both places. What series of readers can you find? Are they progressive or plateau types? If progressive, how many new words do they introduce per book? If plateau, what level do they work at?

2 In the pre-reading stage we try to make the pupils ready for reading. Soon they will have to see how some letters are similar and some letters are different and some are both; e.g., p and q are similar, but also different; p and x are only different. Draw four simple pictures, which could be used as a basis for a pre-reading lesson on finding the similarities and differences in small things.

3 Our eyes, when we read, do not move steadily along the line from word to word. They stop, go on, stop again, and so to the end of the line. Watch the eyes of a quick readers and count how many times he stops per line. Try the same thing with a slow reader. Is there any connection between the number of stops per line and the reading speed?

4 Each time we stop, we read a little before and a little after the place where our eyes stop. In the line below this paragraph one letter is a capital. Look at it with both eyes. Do not move your eyes, but see how many letters to each side of the capital you are able to read. Compare your results with those of a friend. Can you find any connection between the number of stops per line and the number of letters a reader can read without moving his eyes?

tgfapidxsslcvrwjefrAupwmxilkjsorpqkkzbd

FOR THINKING ABOUT

5 Many of the letters of the English alphabet can be written in several different ways, for example

What problems does this cause for pupils who are learning to read? Can any of them be avoided?

6 When we read quickly, especially if we are reading a simple story, we often guess the next sentence and then only look at it very quickly to see if our guess is correct. Can we use this fact to help our students read faster? Can we, for example, teach them how to guess better? What would be the dangers of such a method?

FOR TALKING OR WRITING ABOUT

7 Some of the problems faced by the EFL teacher are also problems for the teacher who is teaching pupils to read their own mother-tongue. What problems are only EFL problems?

8 Even in the mother-tongue, there are frequent cases of reading failure. You will, therefore, meet reading failure in EFL which is not caused by working in a foreign language. What are the probable causes of failure to read satisfactorily? Do you think they can be either prevented or removed? You may want to consider physical, psychological, educational and even cultural causes of reading failure.

LOOK AND SAY

9 The 'look and say' approach to reading gives the pupils a great feeling of success, but it also puts some strain on their memories. For this reason the teacher should not spend a whole lesson on teaching beginners 'look and say' reading. The following suggestions are offered, therefore, as micro-teaching suggestions, though some of them may required as much as fifteen minutes to carry out.

6.2 SUGGESTIONS FOR MICRO-TEACHING

1 The best motivation for learning to read is wanting to know what something says. Here are some notices, etc., which pupils may see and be curious to know the sound and meaning of. Teach them these, and then get them to practise recognizing them when you point to one notice after another, at random:

    (a)   road signs: Stop, Danger, No Entry, ...
    (b)   operating instructions: Press Here, On, Off, Start, ...
    (c)   marks on things in shops: Made in England, ...
    (d)   travel vocabulary: Customs, Passports, Taxi, ...
    (e)   personal names: names of friends written in English, if the script of the pupils' mother-tongue is different
    (f)   medical: Poison, One tablet, . . . times a day, External use only, ...
    (g)   doors: Push, Pull, Exit. Men, Women, ...

2   In small groups you may prefer working with flashcards rather than writing everything on the board. Flashcards can be handled easily. By mixing the cards up you can present the words in a different order each time. You can also remove the ones that have been learnt, and leave the ones which are still causing difficulty. Practise these simple operations. (You will find that if you write the word in small letters in the top corner of the back of the card, as well as on the front, you can hold the flashcard in front of you and look over it at the pupils.)

3   Another exercise you can use is *rapid drill for recognizing words.* After the words have been taught, they should be included in lines containing other items, words which have not yet been taught. Here is an example, for recognizing the word *rubber*:

(a)   book, pen, rubber, cap, newspaper, pencil, window
(b)   dress, shirt, coat, my, rubber, your
(c)
(d)
(e)
(f)   yellow, rich, transistor, parcel, rubber, brandy
(g)   rubber, highway, petrol, dictionary, triumph, shrub
(h)
(i)
(j)
(k)   rub, rubbing, rudder, udder, rubber, runner
(l)   rubber, rugger, upper, bubble, under, rubbed.

In the first few lines of the drill, the word to be recognized is mixed with easy words, none of which look much like *rubber*. The pupil has to glance along each line and point to the word *rubber* each time he sees it. The aim is to be both quick and accurate. For variety, the key word (e.g. *rubber*) should sometimes be left out of a line completely, or appear more than once in the same line.

6.3   SUGGESTIONS FOR THE PREPARATION OF MATERIALS FOR CLASS

1   The drills for rapid word recognition should be duplicated so that they can be handed out to the individual pupils. Not everyone need have the same drill, of course. After finishing one drill, pupils can change papers and do another.

2   Flashcards showing a picture of the item on the top half, and the word on the bottom half, will be needed for presenting and drilling by the 'look and say' method. Either half can be covered, or neither half, as one wishes. Another way is to make

matching sets, half the cards having the pictures, and the other half the words. The pupils then have to match word and picture.

6.4 SUGGESTIONS FOR TEAM TEACHING

1   One trainee can look after the flashcards or do the blackboard work while another drills the words.

2   If flashcards are used, they will be found ideal for small group work, and the class should be divided up into sections, each under one teacher trainee.

6.5 PHONICS (TEACHING READING THROUGH SOUNDS AND SPELLINGS)

1   Before you begin your practice teaching by Phonics, remember that the 'look and say' method and Phonics are closely connected. Take a page of print in your mother-tongue, turn it upside-down and read it. You will find that you read most of the words by instant guessing ('look and say'), but that when you have any difficulty, you start looking at the letters one at a time. After you have been reading upside-down for about five minutes, you will discover two more things:
    (a)   you are starting to look at *syllables*, or at least *letter groups*, in the words that you cannot read by 'look and say' methods
    (b)   you are becoming tired and rather bored.

Remember these two facts when you go into your class – who will be in very much the same position after a short time.

2   Most of the classes you are likely to have for practice teaching will, in fact, already have had some reading practice. It may have been a mixture of 'look and say' and Phonic methods. Your job will be, at least partly, remedial. We therefore suggest that you take one small area at a time and treat it really thoroughly, so that your pupils leave the class really understanding and able to use what you have taught them.

6.5.1 Suggestions for Macro-Teaching

1   Here are some groups of sound–symbol correspondences which you may use as the basis of a lesson. Teach the regular spellings first and the less regular ones later:

(a)	/dʒ/	regular spelling: j		join, jar, job, Jack, Jane
		also:	g[+e]	gentleman, George
			d	soldier
	/h/	regular spelling: h		handkerchief, has, hat, have, he, her, his, husband
		also:	wh	who
(b)	/ɔ/	regular spelling: o		not, strong, doctor, orange
		also:	oh	John
			[w+]a	watch
			[wh+]a	what
	/ɔ:/	regular spelling: or		or, short
		also:	oar	blackboard
			oor	door
			our	your
			eo	George
			a[+ll]	ball, small

2 It is more useful to teach the regular spellings first and then return to the irregular ones. Even if we do this, we are faced with a number of choices about what to teach first. There seems now to be general agreement that the following order is practical and useful:

(a) first consonants of words

(b) rhyming of words (e.g. *ook* in book, look, cook)

(c) vowels in middle position

(d) final consonants

(e) different letters with the same sound; e g. *y* in my, *igh* in thigh, *ie* in tie, etc.

3 Because English spelling is so unphonetic it is impossible to give absolute rules. The following, however, are perhaps more generally acceptable than others:

(a) Most vowel letters have at least two ways of being read, a short and a long (hid, hide).

(b) The short form is the one we use when there is only one vowel letter in a word (bag, beg, big, bog, bug).

(c) The long form is the one we use when the word has only one syllable and ends in a silent *e* (date, these, nine, bone, tune).

(d) The long form is the one we use when there are two vowels together – the long form of the first of these two vowels, that is to say (main, mean, fried, toe).

(e) The consonant sounds are rather easy to make rules about (e.g. *g* is usually soft before *e*).

6.5.2   Suggestions for Preparing Materials for Class

1   If you use flashcards for this lesson, or even if you use only the blackboard, you should make use of colour to point out the similarities in phonic structure of the words on the cards or the board.

2   A simple thing for drilling the different vowel letters can be made by cutting two holes in a large sheet of cardboard and writing a consonant on each side of them. Put a strip, also of cardboard, on which several vowel letters are written, through the two holes. Take care that all the words produced by this visual aid are, in fact, English words, preferably simple ones. (See figure 7.)

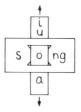

Figure 7

For more information see L. A. Hill and J. M. Ure, *English Sounds and Spellings* and L. A. Hill, *English Sounds and Spellings: Dictation Pieces.*

6.6   RAPID SILENT READING FOR COMPREHENSION

6.6.1   Suggestions for Micro-Teaching

1   Check the eyesight of your pupils. They should be able to read a page of typescript comfortably with either eye at a distance of a metre. If they cannot, they probably need glasses. Even if they cannot, for some reason, get glasses, at least you will know their problem.

2   Check if your pupils move their lips when they are reading their mother-tongue. This slows down silent reading. If the pupils cannot stop the habit naturally, make them hold a pencil between their lips while reading.

3   Another cause of slow reading is stopping too many times as the eye travels along the line. A good reader will stop only two or three times in a line of fifty letters. A bad one may stop as many as twenty times in the same line. You should check your pupils' reading in their mother-tongue. Write five or six lines of about fifty characters each on a postcard. Make a pinhole through it and, from the back, watch their eye as it reads the front. Too many stops show a need for remedial work *in the pupils' mother-tongue* before much can be done in English.

4   Also in the mother-tongue, you should check simple reading speed – how many words per minute the pupil reads. Slow readers read at about 150 words per minute. Good readers read at about 400. One should be able to read silently at least twice as fast as one speaks in ordinary conversation. For most alphabetic scripts, this means that a line of fifty characters should be read in a second. Once again, if the pupil cannot do this in his mother-tongue, there is little hope of his being a fast reader in English.

6.6.2   Suggestions for Macro-Teaching

Our job is to teach and practise four things:

(1)   comprehension
(2)   speed
(3)   remembering, and
(4)   enjoyment of what is read.

COMPREHENSION
1   The more searching the pupil does during his reading, the greater will be his comprehension. We can help him do this by giving him questions before he reads. Either write up the pre-reading questions on the board, or announce them orally.

2   Intelligent expecting and guessing are a great help to comprehension. They can be encouraged by working with material such as a newspaper (the pupils are told to find out what types of sales are going on, what is showing at the cinema, etc.), a railway or airline timetable ("Where do you change if you want to go from X to Y?"), a catalogue ("What is the cheapest size fifteen cotton shirt?") and so on. Cloze technique exercises (see *Lecturer's Book*, 0.4.5) can also be used to develop the useful skill of expecting what may be going to come next. If the pupil expects something to be broken in the next sentence, he will be less likely to understand *window* as *widow*.

SPEED
3   Divide the pupils into pairs facing each other at a desk. Let one read silently while the other moves his ruler down the page from top to bottom, pushing the reader ahead as fast as he can go. Or pupils can work on their own if they are given cards with a hole cut in it as in figure 8. The hole allows the reader

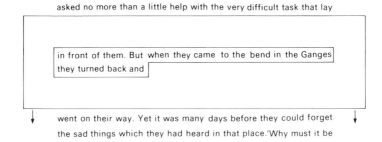

asked no more than a little help with the very difficult task that lay

in front of them. But when they came to the bend in the Ganges they turned back and

went on their way. Yet it was many days before they could forget the sad things which they had heard in that place.'Why must it be

Figure 8

to see the whole of one line and the first two words or so of the next. This simple method will often speed up a slow reader as he moves it down the page.

4   If you have a film-strip projector available, this is a good time to use it. If not, you may use large flashcards instead. You will need about twenty short sentences, each on a separate frame or card. Let the pupils see them in a different order each time. Gradually shorten the length of time for which they are visible. The pupils' reading speed will improve. If you use the film-strip projector, you can prepare your frames using old completely black (overexposed), film, or completely clear (unexposed) film. Scratch the words on the first, and write them with a felt-tipped pen on the second. Neither process is as good as photographing your material, but both are much cheaper.

REMEMBERING

5   The best way to train the pupils to remember the information they read is to give them questions to answer after they have read a piece (but not to allow them to refer to their books while answering them, of course).

ENJOYMENT

6   It is very necessary for the pupils to get satisfaction out of the kind of extensive reading we are discussing here. Pupils will probably always feel that *intensive* reading is 'work', not enjoyment; but we should be able to give them the feeling that wide reading can be an enjoyable habit, so that when they leave

school they will still continue to do it. If we have not managed to make them feel this by the time they leave school, we will have failed in a very important part of their education.

7   Make as good a class library as you can, by collecting suitable books. Even a very small, simple class library is better than none. Give your pupils time, during class hours, to use it. If you cannot get books, you can prepare a number of sheets of cardboard, each with a page of interesting reading stuck on it, so that the pupils can read each card and then pass it on to another pupil during the lesson. Spend time once a week advising the pupils what to read and making sure that they can get it. Older and advanced pupils should keep a note-book for their reading. They can write the title, author and a few words about each piece they read. You should inspect these note-books during the reading period, but you should do so to show your real interest and not for the sake of pointing out mistakes.

6.6.3   Suggestions for Preparing Materials for Class

Exercises **6.6.1.3, 6.6.2.2, 6.6.2.3, 6.6.2.4** and **6.6.2.6** all need at least some of the materials which have been described.

7 Writing

7.1 FORMING THE LETTERS AND NUMBERS

7.1.1 Suggestions for Micro-Teaching

1 The print style of writing is probably the most satisfactory for the pupils to use in the beginning of their English classes, followed by joined-up writing when they have learned to print well. The new teacher must, however, find out what style of Latin writing is used in general by his school. If there is none, he is free to use the print style. If another style is demanded by the school, the teacher should learn what it is and how to write in it himself. Nothing is more confusing for a child than to be caught between two different styles of writing – one is already a great strain on the young hand and eye.

Print: a b c d e f g

Joined-up: abcdefg

2 PUPIL   What's this you have written on my composition, sir?
   TEACHER   It says, "I cannot read your writing."

Having chosen the style(s) of writing he needs, the teacher should practise on the blackboard till he can write quickly and neatly. He should stand at the end of the line he is going to write (unless he is left-handed), begin high up on the board, and keep his elbow close to the board.

3 The teacher should check the pupils' position when they are writing. They should be comfortable, with the elbow of the arm they write with on the desk. Many children write better with the paper turned a little so that the arm sweeps easily over it. The teacher should find out quickly which pupils are left-handed and then ask a left-handed teacher to show them how best to sit. If his class is using ink and the climate is damp, a small sheet of old paper under the hand will keep the paper being written on from becoming damp or – worse – greasy.

7.1.2   Suggestions for Macro-Teaching

1   On the whole, 'a little and often' is the best idea when one is teaching writing. However, nothing can take the place of pupil practice time. Writing lessons should, therefore, not last very long, but they should happen often.

2   If the teacher is given a class of complete beginners for practice teaching, he can follow what is suggested in the *Teacher Trainers' Book*, starting with the first group of capital letters.

3   For later classes, the teacher can review the previous group of letters taught and add one – but not more than one – more. The groups were as follows:

Group 1: I L T F E H   Group 5: i l t u
Group 2: V W X Y N M K Z A   Group 6: n h m p k
Group 3: D P B R J   Group 7: v b w r
Group 4: C G O Q U S   Group 8: c o a d q e
                 Group 9: j y z g x f s

4   After the individual letters have been mastered, the teacher will need several lessons to help his pupils join them up. He should, first teach combinations of two letters, keeping the *second* letter the same, and going through the alphabet with the first letter, e.g.:

$$ab \quad bb \quad cb \quad db$$

Then, still keeping the second letter the same, the teacher should practise three-letter groups in which the first and third are the same, e.g.:

$$aba \quad bbb \quad cbc \quad dbd$$

7.1.3   Suggestions for Preparing Materials for Class

1   The teacher will need a lined blackboard. If he does not have one, he must draw lines each time. Here is a quick way. Take a piece of string three or four millimetres thick and longer than the width of the board. Rub the chalk up and down it several times until the string is well covered with dust. Ask a pupil to hold each end so that the string is tight against the blackboard. Pull the middle of the string a little way out from the board and let it spring back. It will leave a straight line in pale chalk where it hits the board. We suggest that the teacher should use a different coloured chalk from the one he will be writing the letters with. He can be sure of horizontal lines if he marks a series of points about fifteen centimetres apart down each side of the board in ink or pencil. The two pupils will then be better able to place their ends of the string.

2 Good writing makes a difference between thick and thin strokes. The diagonals which move from top right to bottom left are thinner than those which move from top left to bottom right, e.g.:

This is difficult to do with chalk on a blackboard. If, however, the teacher sharpens his chalks – not as one sharpens a pencil, but as one sharpens a chisel – like this:

not   *but*   *or*

the thick and thin strokes will appear naturally. The point wears down rather quickly. We advise preparing five or six chalks sharpened at each end.

3 If the teacher is not confident that he can write quickly and neatly on the board, he should have his material written out on cards, or he should use the 'conceal and reveal' method of hanging a small curtain in front of a part of the blackboard on which he wrote whatever he needed before class began.

Warning: If pupils realize that a good handwriting is something too difficult for even their teacher to produce easily, they too may give up hope.

4 Many cultures consider beautiful handwriting very important. Make use of this fact, if possible, to give your pupils motivation.

7.1.4 Suggestions for Team Teaching

One of the great dangers of handwriting practice is that the pupils may produce the right results by the wrong means. If, for example, the letters *c*, *e*, *h*, *o* and *s* are written with their strokes either made in the wrong order or in the wrong direction, the teacher is not likely to recognize this fact. When, later, the pupils try to join up these badly formed letters, the results will be terrible, but by then it will be too late to do much, except feel sorry that one did not notice it in the early stages. (See figure 9.) If several trainees get together during the writing lesson, they can be of great help in watching *how* the pupils form the letters and correcting those who do so in the wrong way.

A: Correct sequence and direction

B: Incorrect sequence or direction

Results when joined-up writing is attempted

A: Correct sequence and direction

B: Incorrect sequence or direction

Figure 9

For more information see Marion Richardson, *Writing and Writing Patterns*, Books 1–5.

7.2 COPYING

7.2.1 Practical Work

1   (Preparing to teach copying) Continue the following substitution table in all four of the columns, so that all the sentences which can be copied from it make sense and are good English (e.g. you can add to column 1 *Every Thursday*; to column 2, *our class does*; to column 3, *Geography*; and to column 4 *for 45 minutes*):

| On Mondays | we have | History | for our first lesson. |
| Tomorrow | we will study | English | in the afternoon. |

2   (Preparing to teach delayed copying) Choose three pairs of words such as *flower* and *flour* which are pronounced in the same way but spelt differently (see *Lecturer's Book*, 7.4). Fit them into simple sentences. Draw an easy picture to illustrate each sentence à one which could be put on the blackboard in one minute or less.

7.2.2 Suggestions for Micro-Teaching

1   The main difficulty facing the teacher in a copying lesson is how to present the model at the right time and yet hide it when

the pupils are writing. Possibly the simplest way is to write up one phrase at a time, let the pupils concentrate on it, then rub it out and allow them to start writing. He can then write the sentence on the blackboard again so that the pupils can check their work.

2 The trainee should consider using the 'conceal and reveal' method mentioned in **7.1.3.3** above. He can practise this *before* going into class.

7.2.3 Suggestions for Macro-Teaching

The teacher can treat a whole story in the manner described in **7.2.2.1** if he rearranges the sentences in it at random and then writes them on the blackboard. The pupils choose what they think is the first sentence, the teacher rubs it from the board and the pupils write it from memory. Naturally, the teacher must give the pupils a chance to look carefully at the sentence before rubbing it out. He may even point out some of the difficult spellings.

7.2.4 Suggestions for Preparing Materials for Class

The trainee can try to prepare his own passages containing alternatives for delayed copying. He should try to choose stories which interest his own pupils.

7.2.5 Suggestions for Team Teaching

If a few trainees stand round the class while the copying is taking place, they can check how well the pupils are doing it. If the results are poor, they can warn the teacher before he has gone too far and given his pupils too much practice in writing bad English. He can then give them easier material to copy.

7.3 DICTATION

7.3.1 Practical Work

Write a fifty-word dictation piece which will give the pupils drill in the different spellings of the /ou/ sound in English, i.e. using words like *so, low, boat, though*. (You can find examples of such dictations in L. A. Hill's *English Sounds and Spellings: Dictation Pieces*.)

7.3.2 Suggestions for Micro-Teaching

1 The teacher should practise reading his dictation passage at the three different speeds:
(a) at normal conversational speed

(b)   slowly, in word groups, with the punctuation mentioned in the *Lecturer's Book*, 7.5.

(c)   at normal conversational speed, with pauses for corrections.

2   If the teacher is going to use a dictation piece which has not already been marked for dictation, he should mark it as follows:

(a)   He should divide it into sense groups suitable for reading as a whole. Usually a group of words should not contain more than two or three main stresses. He should mark these stresses (′) to help him with his reading. He should also mark with a coloured circle the punctuation which he will give the pupils in the second reading.

(b)   He should mark where he will pause in the third reading to give the pupils time for corrections.

3   In the second reading the teacher will be giving full stops, exclamation marks, quotation marks and question marks, but not commas or apostrophes. He will not give hyphens or capital letters either. The pupils should be quite clear as to what will be given and what will not. The teacher may either tell them what he *will* give, what he will *not* give, or both. Whichever way he chooses, he should practise his explanation now.

7.3.3   Suggestions for Macro-Teaching

1   The teacher can try *Prepared Dictation* as a slight variation. Of course, all dictation must be prepared: the pupils should not be asked to write material which contains unknown items. More direct preparation, however, is also possible. It would be conducted as follows:

(a)   The pupils are told that the dictation piece will deal with a particular spelling problem.

(b)   They are shown the piece, either on the board or in their books. The teacher calls their attention to the various words containing the sound, and how it is spelt each time (e.g. for the /ɔ:/ sound: *chalk, floor, autumn*, etc.). The pupils are given time to study the piece, possibly as homework.

(c)   The dictation is given.

(d)   The piece is again shown to the pupils. The teacher asks them to check each of the words containing the sound one at a time.

2   The same method can, of course, be followed for other problems, such as the punctuation of direct speech, the use of the apostrophe, capitals and contractions (e.g. *don't* and *I'll*).

7.3.4 Suggestions for Preparing Materials for Class

If the teacher has no book of ready-made dictation pieces, his first task will be to write his own. He should limit each piece to about 100 words, and check that all the words in it have been learnt by his pupils. If he has to use words which they do not already know, he should write them on the blackboard before giving the dictation, together with any proper names that occur in the story. He should try to base his piece on some particular spelling-sound correlation that he knows is giving his pupils difficulty. If he is writing his materials week-by-week, he should try to build into each new dictation piece some of the commoner mistakes of the previous week's work.

7.4 SKELETON COMPOSITIONS

7.4.1 Practical Work

Write or choose a simple ten-line story which would interest a group of eleven-year-old boys. Underline ten or fifteen words in it which you would give as a skeleton for a composition. (If you work with a fellow trainee for this exercise, make separate lists and then compare them. You will probably find you have different ideas of what is the 'skeleton'.)

7.4.2 Suggestions for Macro-Teaching

The form of a skeleton composition lesson cannot vary very much. The pupils must first be given the model in some way or other, either orally or in writing. They must have the skeleton before them while writing. Their work must be judged, not only according to how closely they come to the model, but also taking account of the various other possible ways of expressing the same idea. This needs a lot of time.

7.4.3 Suggestions for Preparing Materials for Class

1 In preparing his own pieces for skeleton composition work, the trainee should remember the following principles:

   (a) The *full* version, i.e. the model, should be written first. The skeleton can then be taken from it.
   (b) The subject should interest the trainee's pupils. Usually a short story with a neat ending such as a joke or a surprise is popular with young people.
   (c) The absolute maximum should be 500 words. Pieces may be as short as 200 words, but more than 500 will be difficult for even advanced pupils to finish in a lesson.

(d) In writing the skeleton, it is usual to give the nouns, verbs, adjectives and adverbs. For advanced pupils these should be given without inflexions, e.g. *boy – go – buy – kite* (*The boys went to buy kites*). Other classes should have some indication of tense in the verbs and number in the nouns, e.g. *children – gone – bed* (*The children had gone to bed*).

(e) Usually *have* should be omitted.

(f) All function words (*on, if, the, . . .*) should also be omitted.

(g) The division into paragraphs should be shown. Also all punctuation should be given, but not the capital letters, except for *I*.

(h) Dashes (–) should be put before and after each item in the skeleton. It is then the pupil's job to decide whether the dash means that a word should be supplied or not.

2 If you are preparing your own material, you may like, as a slight variation, to give the parts of each sentence in a random order so that the pupils have to rearrange them in the correct order (e.g. instead of giving – *old gentleman – travel – train – one day –* , you might give – *train – travel – old gentleman – one day –*).

7 4.4 Suggestions for Team Teaching

The things which take a lot of time in a skeleton composition lesson are the various questions which come up after the composition has been written. Pupils sensibly want to know whether the small variations which they have made in the model are good English or not. If the skeletons are well prepared, it is difficult for the pupils to go very far from the model without making a mistake. However, pupils are both clever at finding new ways of doing things and are also anxious not to lose a mark if possible, so there may be a lot of questions. If there is a team of trainees, they can be divided up between pupils' groups to deal with the pupils' questions. When answering questions, it is of course very important to use only language (words, idioms and structures) which the pupils can be expected to understand.

7.5 PICTURE COMPOSITIONS

7.5.1 Practical Work

1 The teacher should choose the set of pictures on which he will base the lesson (e.g. a strip cartoon from a newspaper), checking that the story can be told within the vocabulary, idioms and grammatical structures which the class know. The teacher should list the words, idioms and grammatical structures which he thinks will be useful to his pupils for the composition.

2   He should choose the methods by which he will present (or revise) these items (see chapter 2, above).

3   Then he should practise these (again, see chapter 2).

4   He should list the questions he will use during the oral preparation stage, and make sure that he asks the questions in such a way that the answers come back in the correct form naturally; i.e. if he wants an answer such as, "He opened the window" he must ask, "What did he do then?" not "What has he done in this picture?"

5   He should try to think of the problems which will arise in the actual story-telling. For example, to avoid the necessity for the pupils to keep saying, "The man in the right-hand house" or "The first man who opened his window", the men in a story can be given names (e.g. Mr Brown and Mr Jones). If the trainee practises his questions on his fellow trainees, he will soon find the problems which are likely to arise.

7.5.2   Suggestions for Macro-Teaching

1   As the pupils will be writing the composition after preparation, the teacher should give them directions as to how to set it out. He might suggest, for example, a new paragraph for each picture.

2   Having prepared the whole composition orally, the teacher can then ask the pupils to write it paragraph by paragraph, or picture by picture, stopping each time for the teacher to check what they have written. In this way the same mistake will be less likely to be repeated over and over again.

3   Another variation is for the teacher to write up the model composition as he goes through the oral preparation. The pupils must, of course, be prevented from copying it down. When the whole model is up, the teacher can rub everything out except the problems – difficult spellings, idioms, etc. The pupils can then be given a few minutes to study these. Then the teacher can rub them out too and let the pupils begin to write the composition.

4   It is a good plan to return to a picture composition several weeks after the first writing and, using the same set of pictures, ask the pupils to tell the story in a different way. They may, for example, change the tense originally used, or they may tell the story from the point of view of one of the characters in it.

5   A good follow-up lesson is to give a dictation based on the

composition. You can use (parts of) the model composition mentioned in **3** above.

7.5.3   Suggestions for Preparing Materials for Class

1   No picture, no picture composition. Your first job is to get the necessary pictures for the pupils. The easiest method is with a ready made set of wall pictures. There are several sets which can be bought or you can use a set from a book such as Hill's *Picture Composition Book* or J. B. Heaton's *Composition through Pictures.*

2   A single picture is much less useful than a series which tell a story.

3   If you make your own pictures, you need not put in as much detail as you will find in the printed ones. Once again, stick figures will often be enough. Make sure, however, that you draw your lines thick enough. Thin lines often seem quite clear when you draw them, but disappear as you go further away from the picture.

7.5.4   Suggestions for Team Teaching

If several trainees are available, they can check groups of pupils to see that they are not making mistakes as they write. The paragraph by paragraph method mentioned in **7.5.2.2** above, is very suitable for group work. At the end of each writing period the trainee checks what each member of the group has written. He may choose the best example from his group to be included in a group composition.

7.6   OUTLINE COMPOSITIONS

7.6.1   Suggestions for Micro-Teaching

1   An outline can be a very full one or a very slight one. Both have their uses. Some pupils prefer more freedom within the outline than others do. Try each of the following methods, using a small part of the composition outline for each, to see which fits your pupils best:

(a)   (least control) The teacher writes up on the blackboard only the main points of the outline. He does not ask any questions, but simply tries to make the discussion during the oral preparation follow the outline. This method will probably be unsuccessful with pupils who are used to being led step by step in their thinking.

(b)   (more control) The teacher writes the whole outline on the blackboard and then helps the pupils to work through it orally, explaining any instructions which they do not understand, but in general allowing the outline to be the only basis for the discussion. This method will probably work where pupils are used to class discussions.

(c)   (control and prompting) The teacher writes up the whole outline, as above. He works through it orally, but this time gives the pupils a start on each heading, to build a bridge between the words on the board and the discussion in the class. For instance, after reading out the heading, *The kind of weather that you like* he might say, "Well, I like hot, dry weather. What about you boys?" Or he might give an example of something to which further examples could be added, e.g., "There are many different kinds of weather. Let's see now, snow, rain .... What else?"

(d)   (step by step preparation) The teacher writes up the whole outline, as above. For each heading, he starts the discussion as above, and then gets the pupils to give as many correct complete sentences as possible in the time available. He repeats them, writes some up on the blackboard, and gets several pupils to say others. In short, he makes sure that every pupil is certain of at least one thing he can write correctly in English for each item in the outline. This method is very slow, but may be necessary, at least from time to time.

2   The teacher can practise guiding the discussion along the lines of the outline without actually writing the outline on the board. He himself should have a copy of the outline, of course. However, if he just reads it out from the book, his pupils will find the whole atmosphere of the discussion unnatural. It is better for the teacher to learn the outline and then have only the main headings, such as were used in **7.6.1.1a** above, on a piece of paper which he can look at quickly from time to time.

3   The teacher can practise supplying examples of useful words, phrases and structures for the subject. He should choose a few of them to introduce purposely into the discussion. He will need to have sentences ready which show their meaning clearly.

7.6.2   Suggestions for Macro-Teaching

The teacher should remember what he discovered in **7.6.1.1** above to help him choose the most successful method for his own pupils.

7.6.3   Suggestions for Preparing Materials for Class

1   If the teacher has no ready-made outlines, he can, of course,

make his own. He should keep his outline to 100–150 words, and should not forget to include a small introductory paragraph to give the pupils a setting, a viewpoint from which to look at the subject. He should remember to make several clear points and to list them in a logical order.

2   It is harder to provide a list of useful words and structures, but the teacher can produce a reasonable one if he works through his own outline, making up an oral composition as he goes, and noting down the words, etc. which he needs, but which his pupils will not know. He should not forget that when giving an item, he should include the little extra bits of information which the pupil needs so that he can use it. For example, nouns should be preceded by the article *a/an* if countable, and by *some* if not. Verbs should be marked as transitive or intransitive, and so on.

7.6 4   Composition/Discussion Subjects

FOR THINKING ABOUT

1   In most school-leaving examinations there are essay-type questions. What percentage of the marks do you think is given to the essay question in the English examination? Do you think the total mark for this question is divided up – a certain percentage for what you say and a certain percentage for how you say it? Is such a division possible? Would it be useful? If so, how?

2   What help (e.g. in arranging one's thoughts) might be better given to a pupil in mother-tongue lessons on composition before one begins to write? What help can the English teacher give more efficiently than the mother-tongue teacher?

FOR PRACTICE

3   Here is an outline composition. Try to write two different compositions from it. For the first, use only short sentences and the simplest words you can find. For the second, try to join the ideas together into about six more complex sentences. You may use any vocabulary you think suitable. Do not, of course, add to or change the story in either version.

> Mother sleeping. William, age six, sleeping. William wakes. Plays in kitchen. Breaks milk bottle. Frightened. Sees cat in garden. Calls cat into kitchen. Back to bed. Eyes shut. Mother wakes. Mother throws cat out.

8 Library skills

1   If you have not already done so, get yourself a *notebook* (or a set of cards) and a *dictionary*. Do this *today* if possible. You cannot become a good English teacher if you do not have the minimum tools of your trade. You cannot do the next four exercises without a dictionary.

2   Study the pronunciation key in the front of the dictionary. *Learn by heart* how it works. Check the pronunciation of the following words (and do not forget that pronunciation includes correct stress):

   canal, interesting, industry, character, photographer, whistle.

3   Check each of the following words in your dictionary. For each one ask yourself the following questions:

   (a)   Is it in the dictionary at all?
   (b)   Are several meanings given, or only one?
   (c)   Is the first meaning given the commonest meaning or the earliest meaning?
   (d)   Are you told what part of speech it is?
   (e)   Is there an illustration of it?

   typhoid, pine, silly, fairy, latter, castle, puppy.

   All of these words are fairly common in frequency. Only one of them, however, is in Michael West's *General Service List*. Which one do you think it is? If you can find a copy of the *General Service List* check to see whether you are right.

4   *Lately* is formed from *late* and the 'e' is kept. *Singly* is formed from *single* and the 'e' is left out. What help does your dictionary give you about problems like this? Are there some general rules given at the beginning, or is each adverb listed separately?

5   What ELT magazines are there in your library? For which years?

8.2   SUBJECTS FOR COMPOSITION/DISCUSSION

FOR FINDING OUT

1   If there is a public library in the town where you are, go and see what books it has which are suitable for children, either in the mother-tongue or in English. What would you like to add?

2   In your training college library, which books on the structure of English, or English 'Grammars', are there? Which of them are intended for speakers (or teachers) of English as a foreign language?

3   If your training college library does not have a book which you need, what arrangements, if any, are there for borrowing it from another library? What would be the difficulties in getting it? (Discuss this one with the librarian.)

4   Where is the nearest copy of the complete *Oxford English Dictionary*?

FOR TALKING OR WRITING ABOUT

5   It would be easier for you if all the books which you want for your English methods classes were on the same shelf together. Probably they are not. What would be the advantages and disadvantages of such an arrangement if it were made not only for English, but also for other subjects which the training college teaches?

6   What help can the staff of a training college give the librarian? Discuss such things as buying books, removing books from the library, deciding what to put on the open shelves, and so on. What help can the librarian give the staff in return?

7   If you had to train a class of fourteen-year-old boys to use the library, what things would you teach them and in what order?

9 Lesson planning

9.1 PRACTICAL WORK

We will start with a group of sentence patterns which have to be taught at some time during the course. From them we will choose a sub-group which can be formed into a unit. We will then add pronunciation, reading and writing activities to give the unit variety and to reinforce the grammatical work. From the unit plan we will make a lesson plan. We will not include the actual design of drills and other learning activities. These are dealt with in other parts of this book under the different skills being taught.

1   Eight of the following twelve items could easily be grouped in one unit for teaching purposes. The other four should probably be taught separately:

(a)   There is a blackboard on the wall.
(b)   Would somebody mind cleaning the blackboard?
(c)   I want to clean the blackboard.
(d)   I cleaned the blackboard.
(e)   I wiped the chalk off.
(f)   Did you clean the blackboard?
(g)   Yes, I cleaned the blackboard.
(h)   Yes, I did.
(i)   When did I clean the blackboard?
(j)   I didn't clean the table.
(k)   No, I didn't clean the table.
(l)   No, I didn't.

Start with (d) and choose seven others which might be taught with it in one unit. Look carefully at the *structure* of the sentences. Do not let yourself be confused by what they are saying.

2   Do the eight sentences which you have chosen represent eight different patterns? Or, would you group some of them together for teaching (for example: *Yes, I did* and *No, I didn't*). A book such as A. S. Hornby's *Guide to Patterns and Usage in English* or the introduction (Verb Patterns) to the *Oxford Advanced Learner's Dictionary of Current English* will help you.

After regrouping, how many patterns do you now have for the unit?

3   Here are ten consonant clusters which pupils often find difficult, especially in final position.

/nd/, /nt/, /ns/, /pt/, /ft/, /kl/, /st/, /zd/, /gd/, /gz/

Choose five of them which would be suitable for teaching in the unit. Which of the clusters occur in the patterns you have chosen?

4   What standard of English do you think pupils studying such patterns would have reached? Choose the following four items to include in the unit. Make sure the level of difficulty is suitable:

(a)   a passage for use as prepared dictation
(b)   a passage for intensive reading in class
(c)   a picture composition
(d)   a group activity such as a song, game, or project.

All four should have, if possible, plenty of examples of the patterns or pronunciation items being taught.

5   Give an outline, without details, of a fifteen-minute activity such as a game, a drill or a competition, which would enable you, at the end of the unit, to test the pupils' understanding of and ability to use the patterns.

6   Make a unit plan which includes all the activities and materials you have chosen in the above five exercises. Assume that you have six 45-minute lessons in which to do the job. Assume also that the two short answer patterns, *Yes, I did* and *No, I didn't* have already been taught. They will only need revision during the unit.

7   From the unit plan made in **6** above, choose one lesson and make a lesson plan for it. Remember to include a variety of teaching points, several different kinds of drill, time for revision and for organizing homework, a note on the materials you would need and, above all, a clear statement of the purpose of the lesson (see *Lecturer's Book*, 9.9).

9.2   SUBJECTS FOR COMPOSITION/DISCUSSION

FOR THINKING ABOUT
1   You should allow plenty of time for your plan. There should be time for the unforeseen problem, for the unexpected opportunity, for pupils' questions. You should also prepare more material than you think you will need. How can you prevent these two pieces of advice conflicting with each other?

2 One of the ways of introducing variety into a lesson is to vary the tension (the pressure and anxiety under which pupils work). How, in your country, can you vary the tension while at the same time keeping maximum speed of progress and good discipline?

3 In exercise **9.1**, we built up a unit plan and then worked a lesson plan out from it by starting with the patterns to be taught. Some teachers prefer to build each lesson around one activity, a game, a story, a visual-aid presentation, or something similar which they know is usually successful. Is one approach better than the other? Can they be combined or done in turn? What are the advantages and the dangers of each?

4 By now you will have started some practice teaching, even if only at the micro-teaching stage. Try to remember one occasion when you did badly. Was the cause a matter of the plan, or the way you carried it out? Would you have *done* something different if you had been given a second chance, or would you have *planned* something different?

FOR TALKING OR WRITING ABOUT
5 Some education authorities give the teachers *Teachers' Guides* which tell them how to present, drill and test each day's materials. What are the advantages and disadvantages of such guides?

6 Is it possible in any way for the pupils to take part in the planning of their lessons or units? How?

7 It is very difficult for one teacher to follow a lesson plan left by another teacher. On the other hand, if you are sick, the teacher who takes your place will need some guidance. What *kind* of notes could you leave which would be helpful to somebody who had to take your classes for, say, a week in your absence?

10 Preventing, predicting and correcting mistakes; and corrective courses

10.1 PRACTICAL WORK

The value and difficulty of the following four exercises will depend very much on the nature of your mother-tongue and the structures which it uses to signal meaning.

1 Here are twelve of the more common English tense forms (no passives have been included, nor have any of the *should* or *would* patterns):

   (1) I wait
   (2) I shall wait
   (3) I waited

   (4) I am waiting
   (5) I shall be waiting
   (6) I was waiting

   (7) I have waited
   (8) I shall have waited
   (9) I had waited

  (10) I have been waiting
  (11) I shall have been waiting
  (12) I had been waiting

Beside each of the above, write the equivalent sentences (equivalent in meaning) in your mother-tongue. You will probably find that you have either too many or not enough verb forms to give one to each. If you have twelve, you may find that the twelve are distributed differently. It is unlikely that you will have a one-to-one correspondence.

Study the results carefully. Which areas of the English verb do you predict will cause difficulty for your pupils?

2 Here are twelve examples of the ways in which English uses singular and plural forms of the noun and verb:

   (1) One book
   (2) Two books
   (3) Three books
   (4) Twenty books

   (5) The child is angry.

(6)   The twin is angry.

(7)   The twins are angry.
(8)   The children are angry.

(9)   The crew is sick.
(10) The crew are worried about their families.
(11) A new crew is coming.
(12) Both crews are angry.

As in exercise **1**, write the equivalent sentences or phrases in your mother-tongue, next to each of the twelve examples above. Do the signals for singular and plural work in the same way in the two languages? Do they work in the same way for both nouns and verbs? What areas of difficulty do you predict for your pupils?

3   Here are nine common word-order patterns in English. You need pay attention only to the part of the pattern mentioned in brackets each time:

(1)   We go to the library every evening.
      (position of expressions of place and time)
(2)   When do you go?
      (order in questions beginning with *wh-*)
(3)   We aren't going to tell you.
      (*not* in negative statements)
(4)   Let's talk about something else.
      (*let's* pattern for requests)
(5)   It's important for us to use it.
      (*it* in subject position)
(6)   A book that is on the shelf is useless.
      (a clause qualifying a noun)
(7)   I am reading because I have a test tomorrow.
      (sequence of sentences joined by *because*)
(8)   I myself can see myself failing.
      (*myself* as emphasizer and as object)
(9)   We want our exams marked 'excellent'.
      (*want*+noun+past participle+adjective)

Once again, check whether the word-order of the equivalent sentences *can* be the same in your mother-tongue. We emphasize *can*, because in many languages word-order is one of the more flexible systems of signalling meaning.

4   Here are some examples of the way the comma and the inverted commas are used in English to show direct speech:
"When you go," she added, "you should leave by the back door." She looked at Herring rudely. "You do know where the back door is?" she continued.

"Yes," he answered, "it is the one marked 'Tradesmen', isn't it?"

"I have never noticed; I do not use it."

In each of the sentences, notice the following:

(a) Is an inverted comma used?
(b) Is an ordinary comma used?
(c) Is a full stop used?
(d) Is a capital letter used?
(e) In what order do the inverted commas, ordinary commas, full stops and capital letters occur?
(f) Is a fresh paragraph started and, if so, when?

Are the rules (a) to (f) above the same in the punctuation of direct speech in your mother-tongue? Which of them will give trouble to your pupils?

10.2   SUBJECTS FOR COMPOSITION/DICUSSION

TO FIND OUT

1   Take *one* English preposition, e.g. *off.* How many different meanings for this word can you find? Examples: *Take your coat off. Run off and play. Have you turned off the lights? Five per cent off the price.* How many different prepositions, or other grammatical devices, do you need in your mother-tongue to deal with the list you have produced?

2   Now take one of the prepositions in your mother-tongue which is used to translate a sentence with *off* in English, make a list of its different meanings in your mother-tongue and see how many English prepositions are needed to translate these various meanings in English.

FOR THINKING ABOUT

3   Which common errors caused by mother-tongue interference do you think your pupils will keep longest and have the greatest difficulty in getting rid of? Why?

FOR TALKING OR WRITING ABOUT

4   Before we begin to teach, it is extremely useful to be able to know what kinds of errors our pupils are likely to make. We can get this information by studying a comparison of the English language and their mother-tongue (this is called *contrastive analysis*), or by studying a list of mistakes actually made by pupils whose mother-tongue is the same as our pupils' (this is called *error analysis*). After we have been teaching the same group for a few years, we no longer need it.

Indeed, we could write most of it out of our heads. What administrative arrangements could be made in a large school or a school system to put these two facts together and save a lot of work?

5 If you were to teach your mother-tongue to an Englishman from England, what kinds of cultural problems (problems caused by differences in customs, beliefs, etc.) would you predict which would make it difficult for him to read novels about life in your country?

10.3 CORRECTING PUPILS' MISTAKES

10.3.1 Practical Work

1 The following composition is full of mistakes of all kinds. It would be very difficult to correct as a whole. Try approaching it as follows. Go through it first and draw a circle in pencil round each mistake.

Next go through it again and try to put each mistake into one of the following six categories:

(1) Spelling
(2) Vocabulary
(3) Grammar
    (a) Inflexions
    (b) Patterns
    (c) Idioms
(4) Logical development.

You can do this by writing one of the six numbers above next to the mistake.

Subject given: *All men were born equal. Do you agree?* Give your reasons in about 500 words.

Student's answer:

Before father going we should ask what the word equal means. It does not really mean the same. On a weighting scales two eggs may perhaps equal two small apples, but the eggs and the apples are differing. In the same way two twin boys may seem equal in all respects, but in fact one of them is worried about his examination and the other is not. The boys are the same but not equal.

On other hand the matter of height and weight are not really important. What matters are the possibilities which lie in front of a newborn child. What is possibility for growing up into happy educated adult? Many don't. In this sense men are really not born equal.

It is obvious that all men are not born equally. They have different noses, different jobs, different wives and the different ideas. They did not even came into the world equal. The weight of a baby varies as so do other things like his health, his eye colouring and his parents. Perhaps baby human all look the same to the elefant, just as all baby elefants look prettymuch alike to a human observer. But the mother is not so stupid.

Sometimes where one is born is biggest thing. The writings of Shakespeare have always interested for me very much and I like statistics so I know that two thirds of the world's people live near Starvation. To be born in Clacutta, for example is not a good idea.

In other places is more important what class one is born into. The Rich Families usually give their children better advantages than the poor children. Not always. Rich children are usually spoilt and that is a disavantage.

In future perhaps it will be even better. One of the good things about democracy is that it believed all men are equal and treated them in the same way. More countries are becoming more democratic each year. The communist countries are also increasing. In them, people have to be equal wheather they like it or not. Does it matter if all people have the same advantages? Who knows if happiness depends on things like education. I hate school it never made me happy.

So we may conclude that the united nations have been successful against poverty and disease. And after all whenther they are born equal of not, all men die equal and that is what matters.

2   For each of the six categories give a mark out of ten. Obviously these marks will have to be relative to each other and not to the work of the (unknown) class.

3   Grammatical faults are those numbered 3(a), 3(b) and 3(c) in 1 above. Choose *one* of these categories and write comments to the pupil about it, either point by point or as a whole. Try to make your comments *helpful* to him, so that he can avoid the mistake in future.

10.3.2   Subjects for Composition/Discussion

FOR THINKING ABOUT

1   People whose mother-tongue is English do not usually speak the language in complete sentences, or even with grammatically correct constructions, *all* the time. Why, when a foreign student makes a mistake, do we need to correct him?

2   "I don't have time to keep stopping and correcting my pupils' oral mistakes." What do you think of this remark from a teacher?

3   How should the work of the Corrective Course (see **10.4**, below) fit in with the normal correcting that one has to do during a lesson?

FOR TALKING OR WRITING ABOUT

4   In many subjects a pupil's work is often judged partly in terms of *general appearance*, i.e. legibility, spacing, neatness in making corrections, etc. Is this fair? Is it in any way a test of the things which are meant to be tested? What about written work in English? Should the same standard of general appearance be demanded, and for the same reasons?

5   What principles can you think of on which to grade the seriousness of a pupil's spelling mistakes? If he writes *important instead of *important*, *read* instead of *red*, *hight instead of *height* and *detremental instead of *detrimental*, are all these mistakes equally serious and to be penalized equally?

6   What items would you include on a list which the pupil could use to help him check his written work before handing it in? State what level the list is intended for, and explain why you have chosen each item on it.

10.4   CORRECTIVE COURSES

10.4.1   Practical Work

1   List six common mistakes of pronunciation made by your pupils when speaking English. Try to decide which are the most serious by looking for minimal pairs in English which would be confused as a result of the pupils' error.

2   List six common mistakes of verb form made by your pupils. Which of them are most likely to cause the speaker to be misunderstood?

3   Make a big effort to find out which are *your own* commonest mistakes in English. Use the same principles as in 1 and 2 above to decide which you should attack first. Set yourself a target of one a day for systematic correction.

4   Some errors are very difficult to explain, because the mistake is a complicated one not easily understood by a pupil. Here are some examples:

(a) The thief said the policeman shot first.
     (meaning: the thief, said the policeman, shot first)
(b) *There is the book whom I read.
     (*whom* for *that*, by analogy with "There is the man whom I met.")
(c) *He never hoped he would see her again.
     (misplaced *never*, by analogy with "He never thought he would see her again.")

Instead of correcting such errors, some teachers would make sure that their pupils avoided the construction in future. They might say, about (a) "Always put in the word *that*"; or, about (b), "Use *that* for both people and things"; or, about (c), "Put the *never* with the second verb." Rules like this will limit the pupil's style, but help him to use what he can use correctly.

Can any of the commoner grammar mistakes in English made by your pupils be *avoided*, instead of *corrected*. If so, which and how? (See *Lecturer's Book*, 10.2.)

10.4.2   Subjects for Composition/Discussion

FOR THINKING ABOUT

1   Learning a language is a matter of building up habits. But unlearning a mistake may have to be a conscious business. Is this true? If so, does it mean that every time we have a mistake corrected we have one less habit and one more piece of rule-using to do in future?

2   Some people do not confuse English sounds; they replace them with completely un-English ones. Many speakers of Indian languages, for example, make quite different sounds at the beginning of *thanks* [t̪æŋks] and *tanks* [tæŋks]. Neither initial consonant, however, is an English one. Is this process a mistake? Should it be treated? In all pupils? In a few only? Under what conditions is it worth attention?

3   Sometimes pupils learn to correct their mistake as long as they are in class. Once they go outside, however, they slip back into the old, wrong habits. Is there any way we can help them not to do this? What about a checklist in their notebooks? Re-testing them from time to time without their knowledge? What else can you suggest?

FOR TALKING OR WRITING ABOUT

4   We have stressed the necessity for the teacher to talk very little and allow the pupils to talk a lot in class. Is this true in corrective work? How should teacher-talk and pupil-talk be balanced up at various stages of the corrective course? (See *Lecturer's Book*, 10.3.1.)

5   The commonest mistakes are not always those which cause the most misunderstanding (e.g. *My mother and father do not speaks English*). Should we, nevertheless, correct them as serious mistakes just because they are so common? Since they are so common, will we not have great difficulty in correcting them? Is it worth the effort?

6   Why is it so important to persuade the pupil of the value of corrective work? How can we do this?

7 We have often said that everything that the teacher does should
   be done because it is relevant to his aims. When the aims of
   two courses differ, e.g. when one is spoken English and the
   other is written English, will this make a difference to the
   design of the corrective course? Discuss.

11 Language games, dramatization, poems and songs

11.1 LANGUAGE GAMES AND DRAMATIZATION

11.1.1 Practical Work

1 Prepare two packs of cards for giving the students practice in choosing between (*I think*) *so,* (*I doubt*) *it,* and (*I wonder*) (see *Lecturer's Book*, 11.1). The first pack should contain about thirty statements. The second should have twelve verbs. Try to find three which pattern like *doubt* and three which go like *wonder*. The *think* type is easy to find. When you have made your two packs, practise on a fellow-trainee to make sure they work.

2 List twenty simple common situations suitable for acting out in class (see *Lecturer's Book*, 11.3). You might list such events as the following:

(a) A man is found on a train without a ticket.
(b) A friend whom you thought was dead arrives unexpectedly.

3 Take each situation in the above list and decide what structure could be easily practised in the dialogue. For example, in (a) above, the pattern:

I had	a ticket some money	but now I have	lost it. used it.

might be used. For (b) above, we might put in examples of this pattern:

We	hoped believed	that you were	alive. in hospital somewhere.

11.1.2 Subject for Composition/Discussion

What traditional games in your culture might be adapted for use in the EFL class?

For more information see L. A. Hill and R. D. S. Fielden, *English Language Teaching Games for Adult Students* (Book 1: Elementary; Book 2: Advanced) and W. R. Lee, *Language-Teaching Games and Contests.*

11.2 POEMS

11.2.1 Suggestions for Micro-Teaching

After you have chosen the poem you wish to teach (see **11.2.2** below) you can practise each of the six sections as a micro-teaching unit. Here they are; some of the sections have been subdivided, (1), (2), (3) . . . .

TELLING THE STORY
(1) Go through the poem and list the words and structures which are 'poetic' and which you would not wish your pupils to use in ordinary conversational English. Prepare the explanations which you will use when you introduce these items to your pupils.
(2) Practise presenting whatever visual aids you decide to use. You will need to mark your copy of the poem to remind you where they are to appear.
(3) If you choose a narrative poem (e.g. "Lord Lovell"), practise telling the story *in simple words*, accompanied from time to time by a little mime and gesture. If the poem is not a narrative poem, be sure you can retell it simply and quickly.

ASKING QUESTIONS
After the story is told, but before the poem is read, you should ask questions. Prepare them now. Remember, the questions should not be about *why* the pupils enjoyed the story or what was beautiful about it. The questions should be about the events in the poem and the things the poet says. Try to have some questions at each level of difficulty. (See chapter 14, Tests and Examinations, below.)

READING THE POEM TO THE PUPILS
It is not necessary to learn the poem by heart before reciting it to the pupils. You should, however, know it so well that you can just glance at a line and then pay full attention to the notes you have made on it—where to put the stresses, when to change your speed, and so on. Make sure your copy is properly marked and that you are ready to read the poem as well as you can.

THE PUPILS JOINING IN

This will be harder than you expect. Your aim is to read the poem more and more quietly until the pupils, instead of accompanying you, have taken over, and you are only one voice in the group. At the same time you must keep them in line while they are learning to do this. If you hear that they are breaking the rhythm or not pausing at important breaks between sense groups, you must raise your voice just enough to bring them back again. Ask your fellow trainees to act as a class. You need not tell them to make mistakes on purpose; they will do so anyway. Even native speakers are usually poor at reading a poem in chorus until they have been through it several times with a teacher. Tap the rhythm out on the desk, but do not let the noise become a loud, monotonous, mechanical drum beat.

INDIVIDUAL PUPILS READING THE POEM

You must learn to read the poem under your breath (i.e. in less than a whisper) at the same time as your pupil does. When he starts to go wrong, you will thus be ready to raise your voice and read *the next* few phrases with him correctly. Do *not* stop him, do *not* go back and do *not* make him read again what he has just read. Practise this kind of reading and correction technique with your fellow trainees.

FOLLOWING UP THE POEM

Prepare some interesting homework for the poem you choose, and practise explaining it clearly to your pupils. Consider, as possible kinds of homework:

(1) a description of the character of one of the people in the poem
(2) (for younger pupils) a drawing of an event in the poem, with a verse copied under it
(3) (for older pupils) finding out about the background of the poem or its author
(4) a short dialogue written by the pupils and taken from the poem, for acting in class.

11.2.2   Suggestions for Macro-Teaching

1   If the poem you choose is a short one, you may wish to work through all six of the steps in **11.2.1** in one class period. For a medium-length poem, however, you should divide the work between two lessons. We suggest that in the first place you tell the story and read the poem yourself. In the second you read it again and do the individual and chorus readings by the pupils. If there is a homework period between, the pupils can

reread the poem you have already introduced and read, so as to become familiar with it. If the poem is a long one, such as "Lord Lovell", take three lessons over it:

(a) tell the story
(b) read the poem
(c) make the pupils read the poem.

You will, of course, do other things during the rest of the lesson each time. You will need only fifteen minutes for the poetry work in each lesson.

2 If your pupils are not used to poetry classes, we suggest you start with shorter poems. There are many you can use, but few are suitable from all points of view. Ideally the poem you choose should:

(a) be written in English as near to good colloquial modern English as possible – there should be a minimum of 'poetic' words and phrases;
(b) have an interesting story or subject which is easily understood by the average pupil;
(c) be written in a simple, attractive, regular rhythm;
(d) not be over-sentimental or filled with thoughts and emotions remote from a child's experience;
(e) not require too much explanation and background by the teacher before reading.

Here are a few suggestions for poems:

Short Poems
Monday's Child (anonymous)
The Cow (R. L. Stevenson)
A.E.I.O.U. (Jonathan Swift)
Children, you are very little (R. L. Stevenson)
A Shropshire Lad (A. E. Housman)

Slightly Longer Poems
The Babes in the Wood (anonymous)
The Road not Taken (Robert Frost)
A Strange Meeting (W. H. Davies)
The Way through the Woods (Rudyard Kipling)
The Destruction of Sennacherib (Lord Byron)

Rather Longer Poems
Lord Lovell
Lord Randall
The Fox
The Gypsy

11.2.3   Suggestions for Preparing Materials for Class

You will need copies of whatever poem you choose, for distribution to the pupils. You will also need pictures of the unfamiliar items mentioned in the poem.

11.2.4   Suggestions for Team-Teaching

The teaching of the poem can be divided up between several trainees along the lines suggested in section **11.2.2.1** above.

11.3   SONGS

11.3.1   Suggestions for Micro-Teaching

1   Choose your song, and practise the *short* introduction you will give before teaching it to the pupils.

2   List the unusual or poetic items in it. Decide which items are obsolete (out of date) and therefore to be passed over as quickly as possible, and which are worth teaching. Decide how you will teach them. (See chapter 2 for help with this part.)

3   Practise singing the song, or, if you cannot sing, saying it over rhythmically at the same speed as the recording that you will use in class. Probably you will want to prepare your own tape, using a good singer. If you cannot do this, you should try to find a ready-made tape or record.

4   Practise operating any equipment, tape-recorder or record player which you plan to use.

11.3.2   Suggestions for Macro-Teaching

Use singing as a change from more tiring work. It makes a very good way of ending a difficult lesson, or a week's work. Singing is also something which, if you can do it yourself, you may use when suddenly asked to take another teacher's class.

11.3.3   Suggestions for Preparing Materials for Class

1   If you are able to borrow a tape-recorder for your singing lesson, you can use it in many ways, but do not let it take the place of your own enthusiasm and hard work. Just switching on the tape-recorder and asking the pupils to join in is not only lazy: it is also unlikely to work as a teaching method.

2   If you can sing, then use the tape-recorder to provide the accompaniment or to record the pupils' singing.

3   If you cannot sing or play an instrument, we suggest you ask a friend who can to help you prepare a tape in five sections.

Mark the sections with a wax crayon so that you can find them easily, or note the counter numbers accurately for the same purpose. The five sections should be on the tape in the order in which you will want to use them, as follows:

(a) a good reading of the words without any music
(b) the music alone
(c) a voice singing the words to the music
(d) as (c), with piano or other accompaniment, if wanted
(e) the accompaniment alone.

The pupils will join in during sections (c) and (d). You will use section (e) only after the words and tune are quite familiar to the pupils.

11.3.4 Suggestions for Team-Teaching

Obviously, you must use whatever talents are available. If one trainee can teach the song, another provide the accompaniment and the rest spread themselves round the class to help the pupils with the singing, the lesson will go well.

For more information see W. R. Lee and M. Dodderidge, *Time for a Song: A Book of Songs for Overseas Learners of English.*

12 Audio-visual aids

12.1 VISUAL AIDS

12.1.1 Practical Work

1   If the blackboard is the best visual aid, then your handwriting on it must be of high quality. Write five lines on the board and then ask yourself the following seven questions about what you have written:

   (a)   Is it the kind of handwriting you would like your pupils to use? Do you write in the way you are teaching them to write?

   (b)   Do you write in straight lines?

   (c)   Are your letters all the same size?

   (d)   Is the angle of your letters regular?

   (e)   Are the words spaced out evenly, especially at the end of the line?

   (f)   Do you close up letters which should be closed up, like *a*, *o* and *p* and do you round the tops of letters which should be rounded, like *m*, *n* and *e*?

   (g)   Is your writing free from decorations which, though they may look very pretty, take the attention from the basic qualities of a good (pupil's)handwriting?

   If you cannot answer, 'Yes' to all of these questions, go away and practise.

2   Take a set of coloured chalks and write a few words with each on the board. Which colours seem to stand out? Now go to the back of the room and you will find that some colours fade with distance. Remember which they are.

3   The simplest way to explain the meaning of a word is to show the object it names. Take a wooden pole about two metres long, such as a broom handle, and hang from it, by pieces of string, a dozen items which you might want to use in the same lesson. Put a hook in the middle of the pole (see figure 10).

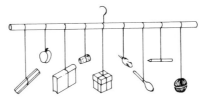

Figure 10

You can wind up the strings (by turning the pole round and round) to store it easily, unwind it and hang it in front of the blackboard for class use.

4 Make a *drill chart* for work with grammatical patterns. This is a sheet of paper or cardboard, about a metre by a metre and a half in size, divided into four, six or, if the class is small enough to see them, eight squares. In each draw two people, animals or objects (see figure 11). You might have, for example, a man

Figure 11

eating food with a fork, a dog chasing a cat, a woman feeding a baby and so on. If you phrase your questions carefully, and ask them while you are pointing at a picture, you can drill a large number of patterns.

You should choose one grammatical pattern and use it for each picture in turn. Then choose another pattern and use that with each picture in turn, e.g.:

He's chasing it into the house.
He's eating his food with a fork.
She's feeding her baby with a spoon.

5 Make a *pocket chart* for Phonic work by sticking two sheets of paper together (see figure 12). You can use this to teach

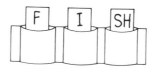

Figure 12

digraphs (two letters which must be read together to corre-
spond to one sound). If, for example, you wished to teach the
digraphs *sh*, *ck*, *th*, *ng* and *ll*, you should write each digraph
on a separate card of a size which will fit into a pocket. Prepare
also cards for the other letters you will need. Then, by replacing
one card at a time, you will be able to give the pupils practice
in reading words containing digraphs. You might start, for
instance, with *f* in the left pocket. After the pupils have read
fish, you would remove the *f* card and insert a *w* card, to give
them the word *wish*. Then you could continue with other
words, e.g.:

   wish – *will* – *wing* – *ring* – *thing* – *thick*.

LOOK AND SAY

6   Use a set of *flash cards* for look and say reading instruction.
Prepare two sets – on one are pictures, and on the other are
the words. You might use the following:

   a dish, a duck, a rock, a ring, a fish, a doll, a sock and
   a sack.

7   Practise using the *blackboard* for *delayed copying*. If you have
two blackboards on different walls, write the model passage on
one and leave the other blank. Ask a pupil to come up, look
at the model, remember a phrase, go to the other board and
write it. Then try another pupil. The pupil who remembers the
longest phrase without making any mistakes is the winner. The
pupils who are watching will be able, of course, to see both
boards and will check for mistakes. If you do not have two
blackboards, you can write the model on the left-hand side of
the one blackboard and ask the pupils to copy it onto the
right-hand side. You will have to make a small cardboard
screen and stick it down the middle of the board with adhesive
tape (see figure 13) so that the pupil cannot still see the original
while he is writing.

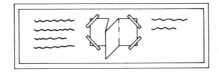

Figure 13

8   You can collect together vocabulary on various subjects at
various levels, and then build stories around these for use with
visual aids.

9 Sooner or later you will need a flannelboard. This is a good time to make one. The simplest kind is a sheet of flannel (preferably a dark colour, since most of your material will be on white paper) about a metre square. This will be pinned up each time you need to use it.

A hinged flannelboard is the best. Find two pieces of thin wood, composition board, or even very stiff cardboard and hinge them down the middle so that together they are the size of the piece of flannel. Stick the flannel right across them, covering, of course, the hinge. The flannelboard may be carried round with the flannel surface inside for protection. Two rings fixed to the top will allow you to hang it up quickly when you need it in class (see figure 14).

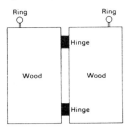

Figure 14

10 Choose, cut out, mount and back with sandpaper twenty items which can be used as a basis for a simple oral composition. Practise putting them up and taking them down in the right order while telling the story.

11 If your training college has a film-strip projector, choose a strip which you think might be used in class and practise the mechanical part of showing it. If you use slides, practise with those. Practise also pointing to parts of a picture with a pencil held in front of the projector lens so that its shadow is thrown on to the picture on the screen. When you feel reasonably confident that you can do these things, try them again, but this time in the way in which you will have to do them in class – in the dark or in a poor light.

12 If you have (or can borrow) a camera which can take transparencies, you can easily make your own slides. If you have a friend who is a more expert photographer than you are, you could get his help.

12.1.2 Suggestions for Team-Teaching

One trainee can operate the film-strip⁴slides⁴overhead projector while the other trainees go round the class seeing how the pupils are getting on.

12.1.3   Subjects for Composition/Discussion

FOR THINKING ABOUT

1   If you do not even have a blackboard, you have still one visual aid – yourself. What use can you make of the clothes you wear, the things you carry in your pockets and the movements you can make with hands, feet and face? You might start by asking a fellow-trainee to put his hands behind his back and then asking him for definitions of words like *spiral, concave* and *horizontal.*

2   Some schools have a visual aids room where they can keep and use whatever they have – a projector, a relief map and so on. Others prefer the teacher to take the item to his classroom and use it there. What are the advantages of each method?

3   If a school is lucky enough to have a film projector, is there any way that it could be used as a visual aid in the teaching of English?

4   Where can good pictures be got in your neighbourhood? Many companies wishing to advertise their services or goods will give away posters if they know that they will be shown to pupils.

5   Children like to help make things. Are there ways in which your pupils might help in the preparation of visual aids? Ask the teachers in the primary schools (especially art teachers if there are any) what materials the children know how to use.

FOR TALKING OR WRITING ABOUT

6   What visual aids are obviously unsuitable in your country? If your are teaching out of doors, for example, the film-strip projector will be impossible to use. What visual aids will be easy to use?

12.2   AUDIO AND AUDIO-VISUAL AIDS

12.2.1   Practical Work

1   Your success in using audio-visual aids will depend on:

(a)   what aids are available and
(b)   how well you use them.

The following exercises are designed to help you with both of these points:

(a) Learn to *use* whatever equipment you can get hold of. Practise until you are completely familiar with the equipment, and can use it without having to think about it.

(b) Make or find a list of whatever audio-visual materials you can find in the training college. Include tapes, records, films, locally available radio programmes and accompanying materials. For radio programmes, you must know the times and the frequencies on which they are broadcast.

(c) For each item listed in (b) above, ask three questions:

– What level of pupils is it suitable for?
– Which of the four skills is it teaching?
– What is the particular aim or teaching point of the item?

Your should be able to do this from the box, booklet or index card in the library which refers to the item.

(d) Choose one item for more intensive study. Listen to it and look at it carefully. Then ask these three questions:

– How would I prepare my pupils for its use?
– How would I fit it into, or use it to replace, a regular class?
– How would I follow up its use in class?

(e) Prepare a short script of about ten questions and answers based on a picture. Try to give the person who answers the questions as much chance as possible to use one particular structure. You might ask, for example, "What is she giving him?", "What is he asking her?", "What is she telling him?", to which the answers might be "She's giving him an envelope", "He's asking her the way", "She's telling him the address."

2 Record the questions on tape, leaving space for the pupil's answers.

For more information see W. R. Lee and Helen Coppen, *Simple Audio-Visual Aids to Foreign Language Teaching*.

13 Textbooks

13.1 PRACTICAL WORK

1 Write out word by word and step by step the advice that a good teacher's book might give you on the presentation of the pattern:

(Please come in.) I asked him to come in.

2 Make a list of a dozen commands which a good teacher's book might suggest to the teacher for *drilling* the pattern:

(Don't come in.) I told him not to come in.

3 Design for yourself two substitution tables which could be used for the question pattern:

What	did	I	tell	her	to	do?
		he		Mary		open?

and for the reported command pattern:

Our teacher	told	me	to	open	that	door.
I		you		shut		window.

Design these substitution tables so that they can be used as a basis for controlled dialogue in class.

4 Visit your training college collection of textbooks for schools, or look in the local bookshop. How many of the textbooks have teacher's guides to go with them? What kind of material do the teacher's guides contain? For exercises **5** to **11** you will need to find two different textbooks, both designed for teaching English to about the same level. The purpose of the following exercises is to compare the two books.

5 Spend not more than two minutes each looking through the textbooks. Form a subjective opinion about which is the better book. Do not ask yourself too many questions about the books. Try instead to imagine that you have to make a quick decision about which book to use next year.

6   Make a clear statement of *your* objectives in teaching English in the class for which the textbooks would be suitable.

7   Check the *objectives* of the two textbooks. How like your textbook/coursebook are they? If no statement of objectives is given in the prefaces, you may have to guess the objectives of the two books by seeing what kinds of activities they provide. Are there, for example, materials for aural/oral work? Is the course obviously a 'crash' course intended to teach as much as possible in the shortest time? Etc.

8   Which book has the better *selection* of items? How many of the items are suited to the purposes of the book? If all items are suitable, which book has the larger selection?

9   Which book *grades* the material better? Check to see if items are well spaced out through the book. Check three or four items which you know are difficult for speakers of your mother-tongue: are they given extra time and materials?

10 Which book has the better *presentation*? Is there, indeed, any real presentation at all? How much space is given to the teaching of new items as against the drilling or testing of those items? If it is assumed that the whole presentation will be done by the teacher, how much help is he given in the early exercises? If there are presentation sections in the book, how far are the situations and contexts which are used real-life ones? How easy would it be to use them in the classroom?

11 It is not easy, without taking a lot of time and trouble to check the rate of *repetition* in a textbook. Use instead the frequency with which revision is provided to estimate which book is better.

    (For the next exercise you will need two readers designed for groups at least one year apart in their study of English.)

12 Make a subjective evaluation of the actual level of difficulty of the two readers.

13.2   SUBJECTS FOR COMPOSITION/DISCUSSION

FOR THINKING ABOUT

1   What *items* in your teaching would you most like to find in a teacher's book?

2   What parts of the lesson (presentation, drilling, written work, etc.) would you most want a teacher's book to advise you about?

3   A good index, particularly one which includes full information about the patterns and vocabulary items in the book, takes a great amount of extra time and space which could otherwise be spent in writing more drills, presentations, etc. Do you think such index writing is worthwhile?

4   The skills of other people besides the author are needed for producing a book. A book is more interesting if it is well illustrated, if the cover design is attractive, the title is well chosen and the size of page and type is suitable. All of these things, however, cost extra money. Which of them seem worth it to you?

FOR FINDING OUT
5   Which textbooks do your pupils like? What is it about them that the pupils like? Are these qualities directly or indirectly related to the value of the book as a teaching book?

FOR TALKING OR WRITING ABOUT
6   If every step is listed and every drill written out in the teacher's book, what is the need for teacher training? Isn't the only thing the teacher must then be trained to do to read the book? Do you agree?

7   Sometimes the teacher's book is in the form of a pupil's book with special pages for the teacher bound in next to each lesson. What are the advantages and disadvantages of this idea?

8   Which would you rather have:

   (a)   a poor pupil's book, containing, perhaps, just reading passages and a few comprehension questions, *and* a good teacher's book

   or

   (b)   a very good pupil's book, containing plenty of material for all parts of the lesson, pictures, drills and tests, *but* with no teacher's book at all?

   Give your reasons for your choice. Would you make the same choice whatever group of pupils (age, ability, mother-tongue, etc.) you were teaching?

9   Who do you think should choose the textbooks for use in a class? If the teacher choses them, is it possible to make sure that, when a pupil moves up from one class to the next, he will find that the new textbook he has to use fits in well with the one he has just finished? If the school chooses them, will pupils who change schools be able to follow through the syllabus without too much disturbance? If the books are chosen by the Ministry of Education, how can teachers with different techniques, or schools with different standards, all use them equally well?

10 Which is better, a textbook which is so large that only by leaving out parts can it be finished in a year, *or* a textbook which, though it covers the syllabus, does not provide enough material for practice? Give your reasons.

14 Tests and examinations

14.1 PRACTICAL WORK

1 To test comprehension of spoken English:
Prepare a ten-question ear-training test (see *Lecturer's Book*, 1.1.3). Each question should have three items, e.g. *men – man – main*, and the pupil should decide whether all three are the same, two of them are the same (and if so, which two), or none of them are the same. Make a score card. Try the test on one of your fellow-trainees.

2 Also to test comprehension of spoken English:
Choose or adapt a short passage for reproduction (see *Lecturer's Book*, chapter 3). Make sure that it contains only the vocabulary and structures one could expect an intermediate pupil to know. Read it twice, slowly, to a fellow-trainee and afterwards ask him to write down as much as he can remember (in his mother-tongue, if he wishes). How much has he missed? He should have missed almost nothing, since his standard should be high. If he has missed much of the story, it is probable that you read it badly. Try again.

3 To test ability to speak English:

(a) Draw six stick-figure pictures, each on a separate card or sheet of paper. The six figures should illustrate clearly a short story, or the development of a situation. First, in your mother-tongue, ask a fellow-trainee to tell you what is happening in the series of pictures. If he is unable to do so in his mother-tongue, your pictures are probably not clear enough. When you are satisfied with them, try them on another fellow-trainee, in English.

(b) Take a simple sentence such as *Pogo saw a friend at the club on Friday*. Then prepare four questions beginning *Who . . .*, *Where . . .*, *Whom . . .*, *When . . .*, so that the answer to each needs the sentence stress to be in a different place. Try them on a fellow-trainee.

4 To test reading comprehension:

(a) Prepare a matching test for vocabulary. There should be twenty vocabulary items in the right-hand column and twenty definitions of those items (in a different order) in the left-hand column. Ask a fellow-trainee to match words and their definitions. If he makes a lot of mistakes, you have probably either given poor definitions, or used items which are too similar. Remove the poor items and replace them with better ones.

(b) Choose three passages from an intermediate or advanced reader. Copy them out, leaving out every fifth word, but leaving a space so that the places where words have been left out can be seen clearly. The three passages should be the same length, or as close to it as possible. Try them on a fellow-trainee to see how long it takes him to get back to the meaning of the original. If the time is about the same for each passage, you can say that this method is a good one for testing reading comprehension. If the time varies from passage to passage, what explanation can you offer?

5   To test ability to write English:

(a) Prepare either a five-item multiple-choice test for correct usage, or a ten-item completion test.

(b) Try the test on a fellow-trainee. What would you do to prevent guessing from having too big an influence on marks in each case? Would the penalties for guessing be different in the two types of test?

(c) If you were using an essay to test your pupils' ability to use English correctly, you might want to set a subject which would give them a chance to show what they could do *with the type of structures recently taught*. For example, "What I would do with a hundred pounds" would be a good subject to set for testing conditional constructions ("If I had a hundred pounds, I would. . . .").

What would be good subjects to set for testing each of the following?

> verbs in the simple past
> *used to* + verb
> reported speech
> relative pronouns

14.2   SUBJECTS FOR COMPOSITION/DISCUSSION

FOR THINKING ABOUT
1   "Almost half my pupils are below average." How would you deal with this remark from a depressed teacher?

FOR TALKING OR WRITING ABOUT

2   "Until the examinations are changed, teachers will go on teaching what they teach at present. As long as teachers go on teaching as they do now, it is not fair to change the examinations."
Is it possible to break this circle? How?

3   What use, if any, are prescribed (set) books? Have they only a literary value? If so, what kinds of question should be set on them? Or do they have a value in the teaching of language? If so, what kinds of question should be set on them? What kinds of question are, in fact, set on them?

Bibliography

Byrne, D. *Progressive Picture Composition*. Longman, 1976.

Heaton, J. B. *Composition through Pictures*. Longman, 1966.

Hill, L. A. *Drills and Tests*. Longman, 1961.

———. *English Sounds and Spellings*. Oxford University Press, 1962.

———. *English Sounds and Spellings: Dictation Pieces*. Oxford University Press, 1964.

———. *English Sounds and Spellings: Tests*. Oxford University Press, 1963.

———. *Free Composition Book*. Oxford University Press, 1966.

———. *Picture Composition Book*. Longman, 1960.

———. *Selected Articles on the Teaching of English as a Foreign Language*. Oxford University Press, 1967.

———. *Stress and Intonation Step by Step: Workbook and Companion*. Oxford University Press, 1965.

Hill, L. A: and Fielden, R. D. S. *English Language Teaching Games for Adult Students*. Book 1: Elementary. Book 2: Advanced. Evans Brothers, 1974.

Lee, W. R. *Language-Teaching Games and Contests*. Oxford University Press, 1965.

Lee, W. R. and Coppen, H. *Simple Audio-Visual Aids to Foreign Language Teaching*. 2nd rev. ed. Oxford University Press, 1968.

Richardson, M. *Writing and Writing Patterns*. Books 1–5. University of London Press, 1935.

West, M. *A General Service List of English Words: with Semantic Frequencies and a Supplementary Word-List for the Writing of Popular Science and Technology*. Rev. ed. Longman, 1953.